Low-Carb Recipes

Low-Carb Recipes

Front Cover

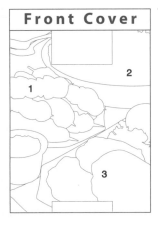

1. Chicken Kabobs, page 49
2. Greek Salad, page 26
3. Turkey Patties, page 51

1. Chocolate Nut Strawberries, page 145
2. Hazelnut Chocolate Torte, page 148

Back Cover

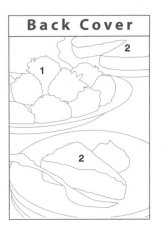

Low-Carb Recipes

Copyright © Company's Coming Publishing Limited

All rights reserved worldwide. No part of this book may be reproduced, stored in a retrieval system or transmitted in any form by any means without written permission in advance from the publisher.

In the case of photocopying or other reprographic copying, a license may be purchased from the Canadian Copyright Licensing Agency (Access Copyright). Visit www.accesscopyright.ca or call toll free 1-800-893-5777. In the United States, please contact the Copyright Clearance Centre at www.copyright.com or call 978-646-8600.

Brief portions of this book may be reproduced for review purposes, provided credit is given to the source. Reviewers are invited to contact the publisher for additional information.

First printing March 2005

Library and Archives Canada Cataloguing in Publication

Paré, Jean
    Low-carb recipes / Jean Paré.

(Lifestyle series)
Includes index.
ISBN 1-896891-71-3

    1. Low-carbohydrate diet—Recipes. I. Title. II. Series: Paré, Jean. Lifestyle series.

RM237.73.P37 2005   641.5'6383   C2004-904529-6

Published by
Company's Coming Publishing Limited
2311 – 96 Street
Edmonton, Alberta, Canada T6N 1G3
Tel: 780-450-6223   Fax: 780-450-1857
www.companyscoming.com

Printed in China

We gratefully acknowledge the following suppliers for their generous support of our Test Kitchen and Photography Studio:

Broil King Barbecues
Corelle ®
Hamilton Beach ® Canada
Lagostina ®
Proctor Silex ® Canada
Tupperware ®

Our special thanks to the following businesses for providing various props for photography:

Anchor Hocking Canada
Canhome Global
Casa Bugatti
Cherison Enterprises Inc.
Danesco Inc.
Dansk Gifts
Emile Henry
Island Pottery Inc.
Klass Works
Lagostina®
Out of the Fire Studio
Pfaltzgraff Canada
Pyrex ® Storage
The Dazzling Gourmet
Totally Bamboo
Wiltshire®

Company's
Coming
COOKBOOKS ®

Company's Coming is a registered trademark owned by Company's Coming Publishing Limited

Visit us on-line

companyscoming.com

| Who We Are | Browse Cookbooks | Cooking Tonight? | Home |

everyday ingredients

feature recipes

feature recipes — Cooking tonight? Check out this month's *feature recipes*—absolutely FREE!

tips and tricks — Looking for some great kitchen helpers? *tips and tricks* is here to save the day!

reader circle — In search of answers to cooking or household questions? Do you have answers you'd like to share? Join the fun with *reader circle*, our on-line question and answer bulletin board. Our *reader circle chat room* connects you with cooks from around the world. Great for swapping recipes too!

cooking links — Other interesting and informative web-sites are just a click away with *cooking links.*

keyword search — Find cookbooks by title, description or food category using *keyword search*.

e-mail us — We want to hear from you—*e-mail us* lets you offer suggestions for upcoming titles, or share your favourite recipes.

Company's Coming
COOKBOOKS®

Canada's
most popular
cookbooks!

Company's Coming cookbooks

ORIGINAL SERIES

150 Delicious Squares
Casseroles
Muffins & More
Salads
Appetizers
Soups & Sandwiches
Cookies
Pasta
Barbecues
Preserves
Chicken, Etc.
Kids Cooking
Cooking For Two
Slow Cooker Recipes

One Dish Meals
Starters
Stir-Fry
Make-Ahead Meals
The Potato Book
Low-Fat Cooking
Low-Fat Pasta
Cook For Kids
Stews, Chilies & Chowders
Fondues
The Beef Book
The Cheese Book
The Rookie Cook
Rush-Hour Recipes

Sweet Cravings
Year-Round Grilling
Garden Greens
Chinese Cooking
The Pork Book
Recipes For Leftovers
The Egg Book
School Days Parties
Herbs & Spices
The Beverage Book
Slow Cooker Dinners
30-Minute Weekday Meals
NEW May 1/05

LIFESTYLE SERIES

Diabetic Cooking
Heart-Friendly Cooking
Diabetic Dinners

MOST LOVED RECIPE COLLECTION

Most Loved Appetizers
Most Loved Main Courses
Most Loved Treats
Most Loved Barbecuing NEW April 1/05

SPECIAL OCCASION SERIES

Gifts from the Kitchen
Weekend Cooking
Baking—Simple to Sensational

Table of contents

The Company's Coming

story

Jean Paré grew up understanding that the combination of family, friends and home cooking is the essence of a good life. From her mother she learned to appreciate good cooking, while her father praised even her earliest attempts. When she left home she took with her many acquired family recipes, a love of cooking and an intriguing desire to read recipe books like novels!

"never share a recipe you wouldn't use yourself"

In 1963, when her four children had all reached school age, Jean volunteered to cater the 50th anniversary of the Vermilion School of Agriculture, now Lakeland College. Working out of her home, Jean prepared a dinner for over 1000 people which launched a flourishing catering operation that continued for over eighteen years. During that time she was provided with countless opportunities to test new ideas with immediate feedback—resulting in empty plates and contented customers! Whether preparing cocktail sandwiches for a house party or serving a hot meal for 1500 people, Jean Paré earned a reputation for good food, courteous service and reasonable prices.

"Why don't you write a cookbook?" Time and again, as requests for her recipes mounted, Jean was asked that question. Jean's response was to team up with her son, Grant Lovig, in the fall of 1980 to form Company's Coming Publishing Limited. April 14, 1981 marked the debut of "150 DELICIOUS SQUARES," the first Company's Coming cookbook in what soon would become Canada's most popular cookbook series.

Jean Paré's operation has grown steadily from the early days of working out of a spare bedroom in her home. Full-time staff includes marketing personnel located in major cities across Canada. Home Office is based in Edmonton, Alberta in a modern building constructed specially for the company.

Today the company distributes throughout Canada and the United States in addition to numerous overseas markets, all under the guidance of Jean's daughter, Gail Lovig. Best-sellers many times over in English, Company's Coming cookbooks have also been published in French and Spanish. Familiar and trusted in home kitchens around the world, Company's Coming cookbooks are offered in a variety of formats, including the original softcover series.

Jean Paré's approach to cooking has always called for quick and easy recipes using everyday ingredients. Even when travelling, she is constantly on the lookout for new ideas to share with her readers. At home, she can usually be found researching and writing recipes, or working in the company's test

kitchen. Jean continues to gain new supporters by adhering to what she calls "the golden rule of cooking:" never share a recipe you wouldn't use yourself. It's an approach that works—*millions of times over!*

foreword

Low-Carb Recipes offers more than 140 delicious recipe ideas for limiting carbohydrates in your daily diet. Choose from a variety of easy-to-prepare, kitchen-tested recipes, every one lower in carbs but not in taste. Whether it suits your plan for a healthy lifestyle or if it's only from time to time, Low-Carb Recipes is a terrific source of great-tasting recipes with fewer carbs.

Many of our favourite foods are loaded with carbohydrates! Cakes, cookies, white breads, pasta and rice, as well as processed foods, all have lots of carbs. But by choosing complex carbohydrates (such as whole grains, legumes and vegetables) over simple carbohydrates (such as fruit, milk and processed foods), we can still eat our favourite foods while reducing our intake of carbs.

The goal of eating low-carb food is to compel the body to use slower-burning fat and protein for fuel, thereby increasing its rate of metabolism, rather than using faster-burning carbohydrates. If this is your goal, Low-Carb Recipes will help get you there. Complex carbohydrates have been chosen over simple carbohydrates whenever possible. Splenda has been used instead of sugar (see detailed explanation on page 9), and limited amounts of healthier fats (such as canola oil, olive oil and butter) have been included where appropriate.

We've created scrumptious meals for breakfast, lunch or dinner, as well as satisfying snacks and tantalizing desserts. Try creamy eggs for breakfast, hearty salads or crisp stir-fries for lunch. Planning dinner? Try some marinated steak, roasted chicken, a thick stew, herbed fish or baked pizza. Hunting for a snack or dessert? Turn to savoury dips and spreads, or rich custards and cheesecakes.

So if your choice of a healthy lifestyle includes fewer carbs, we hope you will include these specially-created, dietitian-evaluated recipes. As you've come to expect from Company's Coming, every recipe is quick and easy and most call for ingredients readily found in your kitchen cupboard. Make Low-Carb Recipes a positive choice for you, your family and whenever company's coming!

Jean Paré

Nutrition Information Guidelines

Each recipe is analyzed using the most current version of the Canadian Nutrient File from Health Canada, which is based on the United States Department of Agriculture (USDA) Nutrient Database.

- If more than one ingredient is listed (such as "hard margarine or butter"), or if a range is given (1 – 2 tsp., 5 – 10 mL), only the first ingredient or first amount is analysed.

- For meat, poultry and fish, the serving size per person is based on the recommended 4 oz. (113 g) uncooked weight (without bone), which is 2 – 3 oz. (57 – 85 g) cooked weight (without bone)— approximately the size of a deck of playing cards.

- Milk used is 1% M.F. (milk fat), unless otherwise stated.

- Cooking oil used is canola oil, unless otherwise stated.

- Ingredients indicating "sprinkle," "optional," or "for garnish" are not included in the nutrition information.

Margaret Ng, B.Sc. (Hon.), M.A.
Registered Dietitian

About Low-Carb

Having a low-carb lifestyle doesn't mean depriving yourself of the foods you love. It means choosing to limit the amount of carbs in your diet: a healthy, flavourful diet you can live with. We've created and kitchen-tested over 140 recipes that contain 15 g or less of carbohydrates in individual dishes and no more than 25 g of carbohydrates in one-dish meals to keep you committed and satisfied.

Low-Carb Facts

Research shows that eating fewer carbohydrates compels the body to burn fat and protein. Carbs are easy for the body to burn so they're the first energy source the body uses, giving that initial satisfaction and "sugar high" that quickly ends with a drop in energy as blood sugar levels rapidly fall. Protein and fat satisfy the body longer because they are slower burning, compelling the metabolism to quicken, requiring more food more often, while still burning calories more efficiently.

Simple And Complex Carbohydrates

Choose complex carbohydrates over simple. Complex carbohydrates include whole grains, legumes and vegetables. Simple carbohydrates include fruit, milk, cake and refined sugar products.

Carbohydrates And Insulin

After a high-carb meal, the body works overtime to convert the carbs into glucose, causing the pancreas to produce more insulin to transfer the glucose to muscles and the liver. If muscle or liver cells are full, excess glucose is stored as fat.

After years of ingesting too many carbohydrates, requiring a lot of insulin, the body can become insulin resistant. Therefore, it takes more insulin to do the same job as before, which can lead to diabetes and obesity. Eating fewer carbs can lower the amount of insulin the body needs, thereby potentially reducing the risk of developing diabetes.

Splenda

We've used Splenda, a sugar substitute, in several of the recipes. Splenda is made from sugar but the body doesn't recognize the sugar molecules, and therefore doesn't digest them, so they don't stimulate the body to release insulin or raise blood sugar.

Fibre

Fibre is a complex carbohydrate that's structured in such a way that the body's digestive system cannot break it down into sugar and absorb it into the bloodstream. Fibre passes directly to the stomach and intestines without stimulating an insulin release. The body feels full without the effects of insulin, making fibre one of the best things to eat when on a low-carb diet.

Health Canada

Canada's Guidelines For Healthy Eating recommends choosing a variety of foods every day from each of the four food groups (grains, dairy, vegetables and fruit, meat and meat alternatives) and including a program of regular exercise for a healthy lifestyle.

Conclusion

Low-carb doesn't mean saying goodbye to carbohydrates, it simply means making better choices about how much and how often they are consumed.

Foods that are lower in carbohydrates include cheese, poultry, eggs, fish and shellfish; vegetables such as lettuce, celery, cucumber, sprouts, garlic, spinach, mushrooms, cabbage, cauliflower, asparagus, avocado, broccoli, green and yellow beans; meat, nuts and seeds; fruit such as strawberries, raspberries, blackberries, kiwifruit, grapefruit, lemons, limes and peaches.

Scrambled Egg Sauté

A spicy start to the day! Zesty tomato with fragrant basil is a delicious way to dress up eggs for breakfast.

Hard margarine (or butter)	1 tbsp.	15 mL
Chopped onion	1 cup	250 mL
Sliced fresh white mushrooms	2 cups	500 mL
Chopped tomato	1 cup	250 mL
Hot pepper sauce	1 tsp.	5 mL
Salt	1/4 tsp.	1 mL
Pepper	1/4 tsp.	1 mL
Large eggs	4	4
Water (or milk)	2 tbsp.	30 mL
Salt, just a pinch		
Hard margarine (or butter)	2 tsp.	10 mL
Grated Parmesan cheese	1/4 cup	60 mL
Chopped fresh basil (optional)	1 tbsp.	15 mL

Melt first amount of margarine in non-stick medium frying pan on medium. Add onion. Cook for 5 to 10 minutes, stirring often, until softened.

Add mushrooms. Cook for about 5 minutes, stirring occasionally, until softened.

Add next 4 ingredients. Heat and stir for about 5 minutes until tomato is softened and liquid is evaporated. Transfer to small bowl. Cover to keep warm.

Beat next 3 ingredients with whisk in separate small bowl until smooth.

Melt second amount of margarine in same frying pan on medium. Pour egg mixture into pan. Reduce heat to medium-low. Stir slowly and constantly with spatula, scraping side and bottom of pan until egg is set. Divide egg between 2 individual plates. Spoon tomato mixture over top of each.

Sprinkle with Parmesan cheese and basil. Serves 2.

1 serving: 362 Calories; 24.4 g Total Fat (11.3 g Mono, 2.7 g Poly, 7.7 g Sat); 441 mg Cholesterol; **16 g Carbohydrate**; 3 g Fibre; 21 g Protein; 859 mg Sodium

Spinach And Bacon Omelet

Delicious and filling. Full of rich, earthy flavours.

Hard margarine (or butter)	1 tbsp.	15 mL
Thinly sliced green onion	1/3 cup	75 mL
Sliced fresh white mushrooms	1/2 cup	125 mL
Canadian back bacon slice (about 1/2 oz., 14 g), cut into thin strips	1	1
Fresh spinach, stems removed, lightly packed	1 cup	250 mL
Large eggs	3	3
Milk	1 tbsp.	15 mL
Salt, just a pinch		
Pepper, just a pinch		
Hard margarine (or butter)	1 tsp.	5 mL
Grated light medium Cheddar cheese	2 tbsp.	30 mL

Melt first amount of margarine in non-stick medium frying pan on medium. Add green onion. Cook for 2 to 3 minutes, stirring often, until softened.

Add mushrooms and bacon. Cook for about 2 minutes, stirring occasionally, until mushrooms are softened.

Add spinach. Heat and stir for about 1 minute until spinach is wilted and liquid is almost evaporated. Transfer to small bowl. Set aside.

Beat next 4 ingredients with whisk in separate small bowl until smooth.

Melt second amount of margarine in same frying pan on medium. Pour egg mixture into pan. Reduce heat to medium-low. When starting to set at outside edge, tilt pan and gently lift cooked egg with spatula, easing around pan from outside edge in. Allow uncooked egg to flow onto bottom of pan. Repeat, working around pan, until egg is softly set.

Sprinkle cheese and spinach mixture on 1/2 of omelet. Fold other 1/2 of omelet over spinach mixture. Cover. Cook for about 2 minutes until cheese is melted. Makes 1 omelet. Serves 2.

1 serving: 267 Calories; 21.3 g Total Fat (11.1 g Mono, 2.3 g Poly, 5.8 g Sat); 333 mg Cholesterol; **5 g Carbohydrate**; 1 g Fibre; 15 g Protein; 379 mg Sodium

Creamy Eggs On Mushrooms

Portobello mushrooms stuffed with a savoury egg filling make a hearty and delicious breakfast.

Olive (or canola) oil	2 tbsp.	30 mL
Garlic clove, minced (or 1/4 tsp., 1 mL, powder)	1	1
Large whole portobello mushrooms (about 5 inch, 12.5 cm, diameter)	4	4
Olive (or canola) oil	1 tbsp.	15 mL
Chopped onion	1/2 cup	125 mL
Diced red pepper	1/2 cup	125 mL
Garlic clove, minced (or 1/4 tsp., 1 mL, powder)	1	1
All-purpose flour	4 tsp.	20 mL
Low-sodium prepared chicken broth	2/3 cup	150 mL
Whipping cream	1/4 cup	60 mL
Large hard-cooked eggs, chopped	4	4
Seasoned salt	1/2 tsp.	2 mL
Dill weed	1/4 tsp.	1 mL
Pepper	1/8 tsp.	0.5 mL
Finely chopped fresh parsley, for garnish	1 tbsp.	15 mL

Combine first amounts of olive oil and garlic in small cup.

Remove mushroom stems with knife. Remove and discard dark gills with spoon. Brush olive oil mixture on both sides of each mushroom. Preheat electric grill for 5 minutes or gas barbecue to medium (see Note). Cook mushrooms on greased grill for about 5 minutes per side until grill marks appear and mushrooms are tender. Transfer to large plate. Cover to keep warm.

Heat second amount of olive oil in large frying pan on medium. Add onion. Cook for 5 to 10 minutes, stirring often, until softened.

Add red pepper and second amount of garlic. Cook for 2 to 3 minutes, stirring often, until red pepper is tender-crisp.

Add flour. Heat and stir for 1 minute.

Slowly add broth and whipping cream, stirring constantly. Heat and stir for about 5 minutes until boiling and thickened.

Add next 4 ingredients. Stir until heated through. Makes 2 cups (500 mL) filling. Divide and spoon into mushroom caps.

(continued on next page)

Sprinkle each with parsley. Makes 4 stuffed mushrooms. Serves 4.

1 serving: 279 Calories; 21.4 g Total Fat (11.1 g Mono, 2 g Poly, 6.3 g Sat);
234 mg Cholesterol; **13 g Carbohydrate**; 3 g Fibre; 11 g Protein; 330 mg Sodium

Pictured on page 17.

Note: Mushrooms may be broiled in oven. Place on greased broiler pan. Broil about
4 inches (10 cm) from heat in oven for about 5 minutes per side until tender.

Eggs Florentine

*An easy breakfast recipe that's still fancy enough for company. A light sprinkling of nutmeg is the
perfect touch!*

Hard margarine (or butter)	2 tsp.	10 mL
Finely chopped onion	1/4 cup	60 mL
Fresh spinach, stems removed, **lightly packed**	1 cup	250 mL
Light sour cream (or milk)	2 tsp.	10 mL
Ground nutmeg, sprinkle		
Salt, just a pinch		
Water, approximately	4 cups	1 L
White vinegar	2 tsp.	10 mL
Large eggs	2	2

Melt margarine in small frying pan on medium. Add onion. Cook for 5 to 10 minutes,
stirring often, until softened.

Add next 4 ingredients. Heat and stir for about 1 minute until spinach is just wilted.
Remove from heat. Cover to keep warm.

Pour water into medium saucepan until 1 1/2 inches (3.8 cm) deep. Add vinegar. Stir.
Bring to a boil on medium-high. Reduce heat to medium. Water should continue to
simmer. Break 1 egg into shallow dish. Slip egg into water. Repeat with remaining egg.
Cook for 2 to 3 minutes until egg whites are set and yolks reach desired doneness.
Spread spinach mixture in centre of individual plate. Carefully remove eggs with
slotted spoon, shaking gently to remove excess liquid. Place on top of spinach
mixture. Serves 1.

1 serving: 257 Calories; 18.7 g Total Fat (9.3 g Mono, 2.3 g Poly, 5.6 g Sat);
433 mg Cholesterol; **8 g Carbohydrate**; 2 g Fibre; 15 g Protein; 269 mg Sodium

Hearty Ham Quiche

Ham for dinner one day, quiche for the next day! This crustless quiche is sure to become a favourite!

Hard margarine (or butter)	2 tsp.	10 mL
Finely diced cooked ham	1 cup	250 mL
Finely chopped cauliflower	1 cup	250 mL
Sliced fresh white mushrooms	1 cup	250 mL
Large eggs	6	6
Milk	3/4 cup	175 mL
All-purpose flour	1 tbsp.	15 mL
Salt	1/8 tsp.	0.5 mL
Pepper	1/2 tsp.	2 mL
Grated Swiss cheese	3/4 cup	175 mL

Melt margarine in large frying pan on medium. Add next 3 ingredients. Cook for 5 to 10 minutes, stirring occasionally, until cauliflower is tender-crisp and mushrooms are starting to brown. Transfer to medium bowl. Cool.

Beat next 5 ingredients with whisk in large bowl until smooth. Add ham mixture. Stir well. Pour into greased 9 inch (22 cm) pie plate.

Sprinkle with cheese. Bake in 350°F (175°C) oven for about 40 minutes until knife inserted in centre comes out clean. Let stand for 10 minutes. Cuts into 6 wedges. Serves 3.

1 serving: 420 Calories; 25.8 g Total Fat (10 g Mono, 2.7 g Poly, 10.7 g Sat); 489 mg Cholesterol; **10 g Carbohydrate**; 1 g Fibre; 36 g Protein; 1117 mg Sodium

Creamy Dill Eggs

Rich, creamy scrambled eggs with a refreshing dill flavour. These go well with sliced fresh tomato.

Hard margarine (or butter)	1 tbsp.	15 mL
Thinly sliced green onion	1/2 cup	125 mL
Large eggs	8	8
Chopped fresh dill (or 1 1/4 tsp., 6 mL, dill weed)	1 1/2 tbsp.	25 mL
Salt	1/4 tsp.	1 mL
Pepper	1/4 tsp.	1 mL
Block of light cream cheese, softened, cut up	4 oz.	125 g

(continued on next page)

Melt margarine in large non-stick frying pan on medium. Add green onion. Cook for 2 to 3 minutes, stirring often, until softened.

Beat next 4 ingredients with whisk in medium bowl until smooth. Add to green onion. Reduce heat to medium-low. Stir slowly and constantly with spatula, scraping side and bottom of pan until egg just starts to set.

Add cream cheese. Cook for about 2 minutes, stirring slowly and constantly, until egg is set and cream cheese is almost melted. Serves 4.

1 serving: 250 Calories; 19 g Total Fat (7.6 g Mono, 1.9 g Poly, 7.2 g Sat); 451 mg Cholesterol; **3 g Carbohydrate**; trace Fibre; 16 g Protein; 528 mg Sodium

Almond Waffles

Subtle almond flavour and crunch make these tender waffles a welcome treat!

Light cream cheese (about 1/4 cup, 60 mL), softened	2 oz.	57 g
Light sour cream	1/4 cup	60 mL
Hard margarine (or butter), melted	2 tbsp.	30 mL
Large eggs	3	3
Almond flavouring	1 tsp.	5 mL
Biscuit mix	2 tbsp.	30 mL
Ground almonds	2 tbsp.	30 mL
Granulated sugar	2 tsp.	10 mL
Baking powder	1/2 tsp.	2 mL

Beat first 5 ingredients in medium bowl until smooth.

Combine remaining 4 ingredients in small bowl. Add to cream cheese mixture. Stir until just moistened. Preheat waffle iron. Pour batter onto greased waffle iron, using about 1/3 cup (75 mL) batter for each waffle. Cook for about 6 minutes until golden brown. Repeat with remaining batter. Makes 4 waffles. Serves 2.

1 serving: 385 Calories; 30.6 g Total Fat (15.3 g Mono, 3.4 g Poly, 11.3 g Sat); 349 mg Cholesterol; **14 g Carbohydrate**; 0 g Fibre; 15 g Protein; 649 mg Sodium

Pictured on page 17.

Sausage Patties

Nicely spiced and juicy. Perfect with Creamy Dill Eggs, page 14.

Water	1 1/2 tsp.	7 mL
Paprika	1/2 tsp.	2 mL
Ground sage	1/2 tsp.	2 mL
Dry mustard	1/2 tsp.	2 mL
Salt	1/4 tsp.	1 mL
Ground allspice	1/8 tsp.	0.5 mL
Ground cloves	1/8 tsp.	0.5 mL
Garlic powder	1/8 tsp.	0.5 mL
Lean ground beef	1/2 lb.	225 g
Lean ground pork	1/2 lb.	225 g
Finely chopped onion	3 tbsp.	50 mL
Canola oil	1/2 tsp.	2 mL

Combine first 8 ingredients in large bowl.

Add ground beef, ground pork and onion. Mix well. Shape mixture into eight 1/2 inch (12 mm) thick patties, using about 1/4 cup (60 mL) for each.

Heat canola oil in large non-stick frying pan on medium. Place 4 patties in pan. Cook for about 5 minutes per side until no longer pink inside. Remove to serving plate. Cover to keep warm. Repeat with remaining 4 patties. Makes 8 patties. Serves 4.

1 serving: 248 Calories; 17.3 g Total Fat (7.7 g Mono, 1.3 g Poly, 6.4 g Sat); 68 mg Cholesterol; **1 g Carbohydrate**; trace Fibre; 21 g Protein; 214 mg Sodium

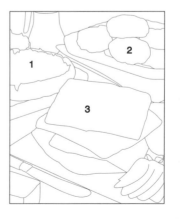

1. Creamy Eggs On Mushrooms, page 12
2. Maple Pork Patties, page 19
3. Almond Waffles, page 15

Maple Pork Patties

Sweet maple flavour accents this delicious alternative to bacon for breakfast.

Thinly sliced green onion	1/4 cup	60 mL
Fine dry bread crumbs	3 tbsp.	50 mL
Chopped fresh parsley (or 1 1/2 tsp., 7 mL, flakes)	2 tbsp.	30 mL
Maple (or maple-flavoured) syrup	2 tsp.	10 mL
Salt	1/4 tsp.	1 mL
Pepper	1/2 tsp.	2 mL
Lean ground pork	1 lb.	454 g
Canola oil	1/2 tsp.	2 mL

Combine first 6 ingredients in medium bowl.

Add ground pork. Mix well. Shape mixture into eight 1/2 inch (12 mm) thick patties, using about 1/4 cup (60 mL) for each.

Heat canola oil in large non-stick frying pan on medium. Place 4 patties in pan. Cook for about 5 minutes per side until no longer pink inside. Remove to serving plate. Cover to keep warm. Repeat with remaining 4 patties. Makes 8 patties. Serves 4.

1 serving: 270 Calories; 17.2 g Total Fat (7.7 g Mono, 1.7 g Poly, 6.2 g Sat); 77 mg Cholesterol; **7 g Carbohydrate**; trace Fibre; 21 g Protein; 252 mg Sodium

Pictured on page 17.

1. Zucchini Frittata, page 20
2. Chicken Artichoke Quiche, page 30
3. Italian Sausage Frittata, page 32

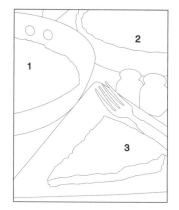

Zucchini Frittata

Cheddar cheese and smoky bacon are a flavourful addition to zucchini. Colourful, too!

Medium zucchini (with peel), halved lengthwise	1	1
Finely chopped onion	1 cup	250 mL
Finely chopped red pepper	1 cup	250 mL
Bacon slices, diced	2	2
Large eggs	8	8
Grated light sharp Cheddar cheese	1/4 cup	60 mL
Salt	1/4 tsp.	1 mL
Pepper	1/4 tsp.	1 mL
Grated light sharp Cheddar cheese	2 tbsp.	30 mL

Remove and discard seeds from zucchini with spoon. Coarsely grate each half.

Heat large non-stick frying pan on medium. Add zucchini and next 3 ingredients. Cook for 5 to 10 minutes, stirring often, until vegetables are softened. Spread evenly in bottom of pan.

Beat next 4 ingredients with whisk in medium bowl. Pour over vegetable mixture. Reduce heat to low. Cover. Cook for 15 to 20 minutes until bottom is golden and top is almost set. Remove from heat.

Sprinkle with second amount of cheese. Broil about 4 inches (10 cm) from heat in oven for 3 to 4 minutes until cheese is melted and frittata is set and browned (see Note). Cuts into 8 wedges. Serves 4.

1 serving: 267 Calories; 17.5 g Total Fat (8.1 g Mono, 2.4 g Poly, 7.5 g Sat); 445 mg Cholesterol; **9 g Carbohydrate**; 2 g Fibre; 18 g Protein; 419 mg Sodium

Pictured on page 18.

Note: To avoid damaging frying pan handle in oven, wrap handle with foil before placing under broiler.

Spinach And Shrimp Soup

Creamy broth, perfectly accented with white wine, makes this soup a special treat.

Fresh (or frozen, thawed) uncooked medium shrimp (with shells)	1 lb.	454 g
Water	7 cups	1.75 L
Dry white (or alcohol-free) wine	1 cup	250 mL
Chopped onion	1/2 cup	125 mL
Chopped carrot	1/2 cup	125 mL
Olive (or canola) oil	1 tbsp.	15 mL
Chopped onion	1 cup	250 mL
Garlic cloves, minced (or 1 tsp., 5 mL, powder)	4	4
All-purpose flour	1 tbsp.	15 mL
Fresh spinach, stems removed, coarsely chopped, lightly packed	6 cups	1.5 L
Chopped fresh parsley (or 1 1/2 tsp., 7 mL, flakes)	2 tbsp.	30 mL
Salt	1 tsp.	5 mL
Can of evaporated milk	5 1/2 oz.	160 mL

Peel and devein shrimp, reserving shells and tails. Coarsely chop shrimp. Transfer to medium bowl. Set aside.

Put reserved shells and tails into large pot or Dutch oven. Add next 4 ingredients. Stir. Bring to a boil on medium-high. Reduce heat to medium. Simmer, uncovered, for 20 minutes, stirring occasionally. Strain through sieve into large bowl. Discard solids. Set liquid aside.

Heat olive oil in same pot on medium. Add second amount of onion. Cook for 5 to 10 minutes, stirring often, until softened.

Add garlic. Heat and stir for 1 to 2 minutes until fragrant.

Add flour. Heat and stir for 1 minute. Slowly add reserved liquid, stirring constantly, until boiling and slightly thickened. Reduce heat to medium-low. Simmer, uncovered, for 5 minutes, stirring occasionally.

Add spinach, parsley and salt. Heat and stir for about 3 minutes until spinach is wilted.

Add shrimp and evaporated milk. Heat and stir on medium-high for about 2 minutes until shrimp turns pink. Makes about 8 cups (2 L) soup. Serves 6.

1 serving: 202 Calories; 6.1 g Total Fat (2.6 g Mono, 0.9 g Poly, 2 g Sat); 110 mg Cholesterol; **12 g Carbohydrate**; 3 g Fibre; 18 g Protein; 581 mg Sodium

Pictured on page 35.

Asparagus Scallop Soup

Creamy, peppery soup with an elegant combination of asparagus and tender scallops. Delicious!

Fresh asparagus, trimmed of tough ends, cut into 1 inch (2.5 cm) pieces	1 lb.	454 g
Prepared vegetable broth	2 cups	500 mL
Half-and-half cream (or homogenized milk)	1 cup	250 mL
Fresh (or frozen, thawed) uncooked small bay scallops (about 4 oz., 113 g)	1/2 cup	125 mL
Grated Parmesan cheese	1/4 cup	60 mL
Salt	1/2 tsp.	2 mL
Pepper	1/4 tsp.	1 mL

Cook asparagus in broth in large saucepan until tender. Remove from heat. Let stand for 5 minutes. Transfer asparagus and 1 cup (250 mL) broth to blender or food processor, reserving remaining broth in saucepan. Process asparagus mixture until smooth. Return to same saucepan. Stir.

Add remaining 5 ingredients. Heat and stir on medium for 3 to 5 minutes until scallops are opaque. Makes about 4 1/2 cups (1.1 L) soup. Serves 4.

1 serving: 164 Calories; 9.2 g Total Fat (2.6 g Mono, 0.5 g Poly, 5.5 g Sat); 35 mg Cholesterol; **9 g Carbohydrate**; 2 g Fibre; 12 g Protein; 1217 mg Sodium

Pictured on page 35.

Artichoke Shrimp Soup

A filling, creamy soup with a sweet, fragrant basil accent. An easy-to-make recipe that's sure to impress.

Hard margarine (or butter)	1 tbsp.	15 mL
Finely chopped onion	1/4 cup	60 mL
Garlic cloves, minced (or 1/2 tsp., 2 mL, powder)	2	2
Can of artichoke hearts, drained, chopped	14 oz.	398 mL
Can of condensed cream of celery soup	10 oz.	284 mL
Low-sodium prepared chicken broth	1 1/2 cups	375 mL
Half-and-half cream (or homogenized milk)	1/2 cup	125 mL
Cooked medium shrimp (about 4 1/2 oz., 127 g), tails removed, chopped	1 cup	250 mL
Chopped fresh basil	1 tbsp.	15 mL

(continued on next page)

Melt margarine in large saucepan on medium. Add onion. Cook for 5 to 10 minutes, stirring often, until softened.

Add garlic and artichoke hearts. Heat and stir for 1 to 2 minutes until garlic is fragrant and mixture is heated through.

Add celery soup and chicken broth. Stir. Cook for about 10 minutes, stirring occasionally, until heated through.

Add cream and shrimp. Heat and stir for about 1 minute until heated through. Transfer to serving bowl.

Sprinkle with basil. Makes about 4 1/2 cups (1.1 L) soup. Serves 4.

1 serving: 195 Calories; 10 g Total Fat (3.7 g Mono, 2.1 g Poly, 3.6 g Sat); 93 mg Cholesterol; **14 g Carbohydrate**; 3 g Fibre; 13 g Protein; 1120 mg Sodium

Pictured on page 35.

BLT Salad

Enjoy the great flavour of a BLT sandwich, with fewer carbs. A light, tangy dressing complements crisp lettuce studded with smoky bacon and tomato. A scrumptious lunch salad.

Head of green leaf lettuce, chopped or torn (about 8 cups, 2 L, lightly packed)	**1**	**1**
Diced tomato	**1 cup**	**250 mL**
Bacon slices, cooked crisp and crumbled	**8**	**8**
CREAMY PEPPER DRESSING		
Low-fat salad dressing (or mayonnaise)	**1/3 cup**	**75 mL**
Apple cider vinegar	**2 tbsp.**	**30 mL**
Minced onion (or 1 tsp., 5 mL, powder)	**2 tbsp.**	**30 mL**
Salt	**1/4 tsp.**	**1 mL**
Pepper	**1/4 – 1/2 tsp.**	**1 – 2 mL**

Put lettuce, tomato and bacon into large bowl. Toss.

Creamy Pepper Dressing: Combine all 5 ingredients in small bowl. Makes about 1/2 cup (125 mL) dressing. Drizzle over lettuce mixture. Toss. Makes about 8 1/2 cups (2.1 L) salad. Serves 4.

1 serving: 164 Calories; 12 g Total Fat (6.1 g Mono, 2.5 g Poly, 2.6 g Sat); 11 mg Cholesterol; **10 g Carbohydrate**; 2 g Fibre; 6 g Protein; 523 mg Sodium

Watercress Salad

A pleasant pairing of peppery watercress and sweet raspberry dressing. Wonderful as a side salad at lunch.

Watercress	**3 cups**	**750 mL**
Chopped seedless watermelon	**1 1/2 cups**	**375 mL**
Goat (chèvre) cheese (about 2 3/4 oz., 78 g), cut up	**1/2 cup**	**125 mL**
Sliced natural almonds, toasted (see Tip, below)	**1/3 cup**	**75 mL**
RASPBERRY DRESSING		
Olive (or canola) oil	**3 tbsp.**	**50 mL**
Raspberry vinegar	**2 tbsp.**	**30 mL**
Dijon mustard	**1 tsp.**	**5 mL**
Granulated sugar	**1 tsp.**	**5 mL**
Salt	**1/4 tsp.**	**1 mL**
Pepper	**1/4 tsp.**	**1 mL**

Put first 4 ingredients into large bowl. Toss gently. Divide and arrange on 4 individual salad plates.

Raspberry Dressing: Combine all 6 ingredients in jar with tight-fitting lid. Shake well. Makes about 1/3 cup (75 mL) dressing. Drizzle over watercress mixture. Makes about 4 cups (1 L) salad. Serves 4.

1 serving: 247 Calories; 21.4 g Total Fat (12.1 g Mono, 2.1 g Poly, 6 g Sat); 16 mg Cholesterol; **9 g Carbohydrate**; 2 g Fibre; 7 g Protein; 283 mg Sodium

To toast nuts, seeds or coconut, spread evenly in ungreased shallow pan. Bake in 350°F (175°C) oven for 5 to 10 minutes, stirring or shaking often, until desired doneness.

Creamy Chicken Salad

This will remind you of Caesar salad, without the garlic! Seasoned grilled chicken makes this a delightful dish for lunch.

Olive (or canola) oil	1 tbsp.	15 mL
Dijon mustard	1 tsp.	5 mL
Lemon pepper	1/2 tsp.	2 mL
Dried crushed chilies	1/2 tsp.	2 mL
Boneless, skinless chicken breast halves	1/2 lb.	225 g
Chopped or torn romaine lettuce, lightly packed	4 cups	1 L
Bacon slices, cooked crisp and crumbled	4	4
PARMESAN DRESSING		
Olive (or canola) oil	1/4 cup	60 mL
Grated Parmesan cheese	1/4 cup	60 mL
Large egg, poached or boiled for 1 minute	1	1
Lemon juice	2 tbsp.	30 mL
Salt	1/8 tsp.	0.5 mL
Pepper	1/8 tsp.	0.5 mL
Shaved Parmesan cheese (optional)	1/4 cup	60 mL
Lemon wedges (optional)	2	2

Combine first 4 ingredients in medium bowl. Add chicken breast halves. Turn until well coated. Preheat electric grill for 5 minutes or gas barbecue to medium (see Note). Cook chicken on greased grill for about 4 minutes per side until no longer pink inside. Remove from heat. Let stand for 5 minutes. Cut across grain into thin slices. Set aside.

Put lettuce and bacon into large bowl. Toss.

Parmesan Dressing: Process first 5 ingredients in blender or food processor until smooth. Makes about 2/3 cup (150 mL) dressing. Drizzle over lettuce mixture. Add chicken. Toss gently.

Sprinkle with second amount of Parmesan cheese. Squeeze lemon over top. Makes about 4 1/2 cups (1.1 L) salad. Serves 3.

1 serving: 504 Calories; 37.9 g Total Fat (22.5 g Mono, 3.4 g Poly, 9.6 g Sat); 149 mg Cholesterol; **5 g Carbohydrate**; 2 g Fibre; 36 g Protein; 653 mg Sodium

Note: Chicken may be broiled in oven. Place on greased broiler pan. Broil about 4 inches (10 cm) from heat in oven for about 4 minutes per side until no longer pink inside.

Greek Salad

A twist on the traditional Greek salad that will have everyone wanting more. Colourful and zesty!

Chopped or torn romaine lettuce, lightly packed	3 cups	750 mL
Sliced English cucumber (with peel)	1 cup	250 mL
Feta cheese, cut into 1/2 inch (12 mm) cubes	8 oz.	225 g
Medium tomatoes, chopped	3	3
Thinly sliced red onion	1/2 cup	125 mL
Pine nuts, toasted (see Tip, page 24)	1/4 cup	60 mL
Kalamata olives (Greek)	16	16
LEMON DILL DRESSING		
Olive (or canola) oil	1/4 cup	60 mL
Lemon juice	2 tbsp.	30 mL
Chopped fresh dill (or 3/4 tsp., 4 mL, dill weed)	1 tbsp.	15 mL
Garlic clove, minced (or 1/4 tsp., 1 mL, powder)	1	1
Granulated sugar	1/4 tsp.	1 mL
Salt	1/4 tsp.	1 mL
Pepper	1/4 tsp.	1 mL

Put first 7 ingredients into extra-large bowl. Toss.

Lemon Dill Dressing: Combine all 7 ingredients in jar with tight-fitting lid. Shake well. Makes about 1/2 cup (125 mL) dressing. Drizzle over lettuce mixture. Toss. Makes about 9 cups (2.25 L) salad. Serves 4.

1 serving: 398 Calories; 34.5 g Total Fat (16.8 g Mono, 4.2 g Poly, 11.8 g Sat); 52 mg Cholesterol; **14 g Carbohydrate**; 5 g Fibre; 13 g Protein; 965 mg Sodium

Pictured on front cover.

Chinese Cabbage Salad

A crunchy salad with a satisfying sesame flavour everyone is sure to love.

Finely shredded suey choy (Chinese cabbage), lightly packed	4 cups	1 L
Thinly sliced English cucumber (halved lengthwise and cut diagonally)	1 1/2 cups	375 mL
Carrot, peeled into 4 inch (10 cm) long ribbons with vegetable peeler	1 cup	250 mL
Thinly sliced celery (cut diagonally)	1/2 cup	125 mL
Green onions, thinly sliced	2	2
RICE VINEGAR DRESSING		
Rice vinegar	1/4 cup	60 mL
Granulated sugar	2 tbsp.	30 mL
Canola oil	1 1/2 tbsp.	25 mL
Low-sodium soy sauce	1 tbsp.	15 mL
Sweet chili sauce	1 tbsp.	15 mL
Sesame oil, for flavour	1 1/2 tsp.	7 mL
Dried crushed chilies (optional)	1/16 tsp.	0.5 mL
Sesame seeds, toasted (see Tip, page 24)	2 tsp.	10 mL

Put first 5 ingredients into large bowl. Toss.

Rice Vinegar Dressing: Combine first 7 ingredients in jar with tight-fitting lid. Shake well. Makes about 1/2 cup (125 mL) dressing. Drizzle over cabbage mixture. Toss.

Sprinkle with sesame seeds. Makes about 6 cups (1.5 L) salad. Serves 4.

1 serving: 134 Calories; 8 g Total Fat (4.1 g Mono, 2.7 g Poly, 0.8 g Sat); 0 mg Cholesterol; **15 g Carbohydrate**; 2 g Fibre; 2 g Protein; 210 mg Sodium

Shrimp And Avocado Salad

An elegant salad—just right for company. The refreshing, slightly sweet dressing is lovely with spinach and succulent shrimp.

Fresh spinach, stems removed, lightly packed	**2 cups**	**500 mL**
Cooked large shrimp, tails removed	**3/4 lb.**	**340 g**
Ripe large avocado, cut into 1/2 inch (12 mm) cubes	**1**	**1**
Pistachios, shelled and toasted (see Tip, page 24)	**1/4 cup**	**60 mL**
Thinly sliced green onion	**1/4 cup**	**60 mL**
WHITE WINE VINAIGRETTE		
Canola oil	**3 tbsp.**	**50 mL**
White wine vinegar	**2 tbsp.**	**30 mL**
Grated Parmesan cheese	**2 tbsp.**	**30 mL**
Low-calorie sweetener (Splenda)	**1 tbsp.**	**15 mL**
Grated Parmesan cheese (optional)	**2 tbsp.**	**30 mL**

Put first 5 ingredients into large bowl. Toss gently.

White Wine Vinaigrette: Combine first 4 ingredients in jar with tight-fitting lid. Shake well. Makes about 1/3 cup (75 mL) dressing. Drizzle over spinach mixture. Toss gently.

Sprinkle with second amount of Parmesan cheese. Makes about 6 cups (1.5 L) salad. Serves 4.

1 serving: 333 Calories; 25 g Total Fat (14.5 g Mono, 5.3 g Poly, 3.4 g Sat); 124 mg Cholesterol; **9 g Carbohydrate**; 3 g Fibre; 21 g Protein; 207 mg Sodium

Tomato Tuna Salad

A simply sensational salad that will remind you of antipasto. Fresh, light and full of tantalizing good taste!

Medium tomatoes, chopped	**4**	**4**
Can of white tuna packed in water, drained and flaked	**6 1/2 oz.**	**184 g**
Chopped red onion	**1/2 cup**	**125 mL**
Chopped kalamata olives (Greek)	**1/4 cup**	**60 mL**
Chopped fresh basil	**3 tbsp.**	**50 mL**
OIL AND VINEGAR DRESSING		
Red wine vinegar	**3 tbsp.**	**50 mL**
Olive (or canola) oil	**2 tbsp.**	**30 mL**
Salt, sprinkle		
Pepper	**1/8 tsp.**	**0.5 mL**

(continued on next page)

Put first 5 ingredients into large bowl. Toss.

Oil And Vinegar Dressing: Combine all 4 ingredients in jar with tight-fitting lid. Shake well. Makes about 1/4 cup (60 mL) dressing. Drizzle over tomato mixture. Toss. Makes about 4 cups (1 L) salad. Serves 2.

1 serving: 305 Calories; 18.1 g Total Fat (11.7 g Mono, 2.5 g Poly, 2.7 g Sat); 32 mg Cholesterol; **17 g Carbohydrate**; 4 g Fibre; 21 g Protein; 410 mg Sodium

Pictured on page 72.

Spicy Broccoli And Tofu

Asian-flavoured dish with some heat. A colourful and appealing choice for lunch.

Prepared vegetable broth	1/2 cup	125 mL
Low-sodium soy sauce	2 tbsp.	30 mL
Cornstarch	2 tsp.	10 mL
Sesame oil, for flavour	2 tsp.	10 mL
Dried crushed chilies	1/4 tsp.	1 mL
Broccoli florets	4 cups	1 L
Prepared vegetable broth	1/4 cup	60 mL
Finely grated, peeled gingerroot	2 tsp.	10 mL
Garlic cloves, minced (or 1/2 tsp., 2 mL, powder)	2	2
Firm tofu, drained, cut into 1/2 inch (12 mm) cubes	1 1/4 cups	300 mL
Sesame seeds, toasted (see Tip, page 24)	2 tsp.	10 mL

Combine first 5 ingredients in small bowl. Set aside.

Heat wok or large frying pan on medium-high until very hot. Add next 4 ingredients. Stir. Cover. Cook for 2 to 3 minutes until broccoli is just tender-crisp.

Add tofu. Stir-fry until heated through. Stir cornstarch mixture. Slowly add to tofu mixture, stirring constantly, until sauce is boiling and slightly thickened. Transfer to serving dish.

Sprinkle with sesame seeds. Serves 4.

1 serving: 192 Calories; 10.8 g Total Fat (2.9 g Mono, 5.6 g Poly, 1.6 g Sat); 0 mg Cholesterol; **11 g Carbohydrate**; 3 g Fibre; 17 g Protein; 440 mg Sodium

Chicken Artichoke Quiche

Mildly flavoured, rich, crustless quiche. A tasty way to use up leftover chicken for lunch.

Milk	1 1/4 cups	300 mL
Large eggs	3	3
All-purpose flour	1/3 cup	75 mL
Salt	1/4 tsp.	1 mL
Pepper	1/4 tsp.	1 mL
Chopped cooked chicken (about 8 oz., 225 g)	1 1/4 cups	300 mL
Jar of marinated artichokes, drained, chopped	6 oz.	170 mL
Grated light sharp Cheddar cheese	1/2 cup	125 mL
Grated Parmesan cheese	1/3 cup	75 mL
Thinly sliced green onion	3 tbsp.	50 mL
Chopped fresh basil (or 1 1/2 tsp., 7 mL, dried)	2 tbsp.	30 mL

Beat first 5 ingredients with whisk in large bowl until smooth.

Add remaining 6 ingredients. Stir well. Pour into greased 9 inch (22 cm) pie plate. Bake in 325°F (160°C) oven for about 50 minutes until knife inserted in centre comes out clean. Let stand for 10 minutes. Cuts into 6 wedges. Serves 3.

1 serving: 412 Calories; 15.4 g Total Fat (5 g Mono, 1.3 g Poly, 7.5 g Sat); 305 mg Cholesterol; **22 g Carbohydrate**; 2 g Fibre; 44 g Protein; 761 mg Sodium

Pictured on page 18.

Spring Casserole

An attractive dish to set before company. Makes a great light lunch or dinner.

Fresh asparagus, trimmed of tough ends, cut into 2 inch (5 cm) pieces	**1 1/2 lbs.**	**680 g**
Water		
All-purpose flour	**2 tbsp.**	**30 mL**
Salt	**1/4 tsp.**	**1 mL**
Milk	**1 cup**	**250 mL**
Grated light sharp Cheddar cheese	**1 cup**	**250 mL**
Cayenne pepper	**1/8 tsp.**	**0.5 mL**
Large hard-cooked eggs, chopped	**4**	**4**
Sliced blanched almonds, toasted (see Tip, page 24)	**1/2 cup**	**125 mL**
Hard margarine (or butter)	**1 tbsp.**	**15 mL**
Fine dry bread crumbs	**1/4 cup**	**60 mL**

Cook asparagus in water in large saucepan until tender-crisp. Drain. Set aside.

Combine flour and salt in medium saucepan. Slowly add milk, stirring constantly, until smooth. Heat and stir on medium until boiling and thickened.

Add cheese and cayenne pepper. Heat and stir until cheese is melted. Remove from heat.

Layer 1/2 of asparagus, 1/2 of egg, 1/2 of cheese mixture and 1/2 of almonds, in order given, in greased 2 quart (2 L) casserole. Repeat with remaining half of ingredients.

Melt margarine in small saucepan. Add bread crumbs. Stir well. Sprinkle over almonds. Cook, uncovered, in 350°F (175°C) oven for about 40 minutes until heated through. Serves 4.

1 serving: 380 Calories; 22.9 g Total Fat (10.8 g Mono, 2.9 g Poly, 7.3 g Sat); 236 mg Cholesterol; **22 g Carbohydrate**; 4 g Fibre; 23 g Protein; 534 mg Sodium

Italian Sausage Frittata

A golden frittata full of spicy sausage and colourful vegetables.

Hot Italian sausages (about 1/2 lb., 225 g), casings removed, chopped	3	3
Canola oil	1 tsp.	5 mL
Chopped green pepper	1 cup	250 mL
Garlic cloves, minced (or 1/2 tsp., 2 mL, powder), optional	2	2
Large eggs	8	8
Ricotta cheese	1/2 cup	125 mL
Salt	1/4 tsp.	1 mL
Pepper	1/4 tsp.	1 mL
Small tomato, sliced	1	1
Grated Parmesan cheese	1/4 cup	60 mL
Grated part-skim mozzarella cheese	1/4 cup	60 mL

Cook sausage in large non-stick frying pan on medium-high for about 5 minutes, stirring occasionally, until browned. Remove to small bowl. Set aside. Remove and discard drippings from pan.

Heat canola oil in same frying pan on medium. Add green pepper and garlic. Cook for 2 to 3 minutes, stirring often, until green pepper is softened. Reduce heat to medium-low. Add sausage. Stir. Spread sausage mixture evenly in bottom of frying pan.

Beat next 4 ingredients with whisk in medium bowl until well combined. Pour over sausage mixture. Reduce heat to low. Cover. Cook for about 5 minutes until bottom is golden and top is almost set. Remove from heat.

Arrange tomato slices evenly around edge of frittata. Sprinkle both cheeses over top. Broil about 4 inches (10 cm) from heat in oven for 3 to 4 minutes until frittata is browned and set (see Note). Cuts into 8 wedges. Serves 4.

1 serving: 367 Calories; 25.6 g Total Fat (8.4 g Mono, 2.9 g Poly, 10.3 g Sat); 478 mg Cholesterol; **7 g Carbohydrate**; 1 g Fibre; 27 g Protein; 709 mg Sodium

Pictured on page 18.

Note: To avoid damaging frying pan handle in oven, wrap handle with foil before placing under broiler.

Beef With Three Mushrooms

A dish for mushroom lovers! The Asian-style sauce makes a delicious difference.

Low-sodium prepared beef broth	1/3 cup	75 mL
Cornstarch	1 tsp.	5 mL
Black bean sauce (pourable)	1/3 cup	75 mL
Dry sherry	1 tbsp.	15 mL
Chili paste (sambal oelek)	1/2 tsp.	2 mL
Beef top sirloin steak, cut across grain into 1/8 inch (3 mm) thick slices (see Tip, page 43)	1 lb.	454 g
Canola oil	1 tbsp.	15 mL
Canola oil	1 tbsp.	15 mL
Can of Chinese straw mushrooms, rinsed well and drained (see Note)	14 oz.	398 mL
Fresh shiitake mushrooms, stems removed, caps sliced	3/4 cup	175 mL
Fresh brown (or white) mushrooms, quartered	3/4 cup	175 mL
Finely grated, peeled gingerroot	1 tbsp.	15 mL
Garlic cloves, minced (or 1/2 tsp., 2 mL, powder)	2	2
Green onions, sliced	2	2

Stir broth into cornstarch in 1 cup (250 mL) liquid measure until smooth. Add next 3 ingredients. Stir. Set aside.

Cut beef slices into 2 inch (5 cm) long strips. Heat wok or large frying pan on medium-high until very hot. Add first amount of canola oil. Add beef. Stir-fry for 2 to 3 minutes until desired doneness. Remove to medium bowl. Set aside.

Heat second amount of canola oil in same wok. Add next 5 ingredients. Stir-fry for about 4 minutes until mushrooms are tender and liquid is evaporated. Add beef. Stir broth mixture. Add to beef mixture. Heat and stir until sauce is boiling and thickened. Transfer to serving dish.

Sprinkle with green onion. Serves 4.

1 serving: 289 Calories; 15.3 g Total Fat (7.2 g Mono, 2 g Poly, 4.5 g Sat); 56 mg Cholesterol; **13 g Carbohydrate**; 3 g Fibre; 25 g Protein; 1021 mg Sodium

Note: Canned straw mushrooms can have a metallic taste. Rinse them well. If you prefer, omit straw mushrooms and use 3/4 cup (175 mL) small fresh white mushrooms.

Skewered Meatballs

Serve with Greek Salad, page 26, or Cucumber Salsa, page 79.

Finely chopped onion	1/4 cup	60 mL
Large egg, fork-beaten	1	1
Garlic cloves, minced (or 3/4 tsp., 4 mL, powder)	3	3
Ground cumin	1 1/2 tsp.	7 mL
Ground cinnamon	1 tsp.	5 mL
Ground ginger	1/2 tsp.	2 mL
Cayenne pepper	1/4 tsp.	1 mL
Salt	1 tsp.	5 mL
Pepper	1/2 tsp.	2 mL
Lean ground beef	1 lb.	454 g
Bamboo skewers (8 inch, 20 cm, length), soaked in water for 10 minutes	4	4

Combine first 9 ingredients in large bowl.

Add ground beef. Mix well. Divide mixture into 20 equal portions. Roll each portion into a ball.

Thread 5 meatballs onto each skewer. Place skewers on greased broiler pan. Broil about 4 inches (10 cm) from heat in oven for 15 to 20 minutes, turning occasionally, until meatballs are no longer pink inside. Makes 4 skewers. Serves 4.

1 serving: 277 Calories; 18.6 g Total Fat (7.9 g Mono, 0.9 g Poly, 7.2 g Sat); 118 mg Cholesterol; **3 g Carbohydrate**; trace Fibre; 23 g Protein; 686 mg Sodium

1. Asparagus Scallop Soup, page 22
2. Spinach And Shrimp Soup, page 21
3. Artichoke Shrimp Soup, page 22

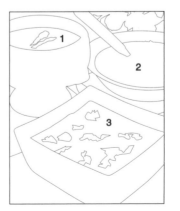

Marinated Flank Steak

This can be cooked on the barbecue, if desired. Leftovers are delicious tossed with your favourite greens.

SOY LIME MARINADE		
Can of condensed beef consommé	**10 oz.**	**284 mL**
Low-sodium soy sauce	**1/3 cup**	**75 mL**
Chopped green onion	**1/4 cup**	**60 mL**
Lime juice	**2 tbsp.**	**30 mL**
Brown sugar, packed	**2 tbsp.**	**30 mL**
Seasoned salt	**1 tsp.**	**5 mL**
Garlic clove, minced (or 1/4 tsp., 1 mL, powder)	**1**	**1**
Beef flank steak	**1 1/2 lbs.**	**680 g**
Beer	**1 cup**	**250 mL**

Soy Lime Marinade: Combine first 7 ingredients in small bowl. Makes about 1 1/2 cups (375 mL) marinade.

Place steak in large shallow baking dish. Pour marinade over top. Turn until coated.

Pour beer over steak. Do not turn. Cover. Marinate in refrigerator for at least 6 hours or overnight. Drain and discard marinade. Place steak on greased broiler pan. Broil about 4 inches (10 cm) from heat in over for 6 to 8 minutes per side until desired doneness. Cut steak diagonally into 1/4 inch (6 mm) thick slices. Serves 6.

1 serving: 221 Calories; 10.1 g Total Fat (4.2 g Mono, 0.4 g Poly, 4.3 g Sat); 48 mg Cholesterol; **4 g Carbohydrate**; trace Fibre; 26 g Protein; 545 mg Sodium

1. Stuffed Peppers, page 39
2. Crisp Minted Salad, page 40
3. Spinach Taco Salad, page 46

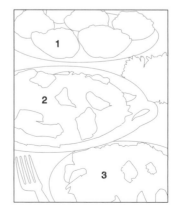

Blue Cheese Steaks

Tender pan-fried steaks drizzled with a creamy, pungent blue cheese sauce. Quick and easy to make.

Canola oil	2 tsp.	10 mL
Beef strip loin steaks (about 8 oz., 225 g, each)	2	2
All-purpose flour	2 tsp.	10 mL
Low-sodium prepared beef broth	1/3 cup	75 mL
Milk (or half-and-half cream)	1/3 cup	75 mL
Brandy (or 1/4 tsp., 1 mL, brandy flavouring)	2 tbsp.	30 mL
Crumbled blue cheese (about 2 oz., 57 g)	1/2 cup	125 mL
Salt, sprinkle		
Pepper, sprinkle		

Heat canola oil in medium frying pan on medium. Add steaks. Cook for 4 to 6 minutes per side until desired doneness. Remove to large plate. Cover to keep warm.

Measure flour into same frying pan. Heat and stir for 1 minute. Slowly add broth, stirring constantly, until smooth. Add milk and brandy. Heat and stir for 2 to 3 minutes until boiling and slightly thickened.

Add cheese. Heat and stir until cheese is melted. Sprinkle with salt and pepper. Stir. Remove from heat. Cut each steak in half. Place 1 half on each of 4 individual plates. Drizzle sauce over each. Serves 4.

1 serving: 378 Calories; 26.1 g Total Fat (10.8 g Mono, 1.5 g Poly, 11.2 g Sat); 75 mg Cholesterol; **3 g Carbohydrate**; trace Fibre; 28 g Protein; 373 mg Sodium

Stuffed Peppers

Chili-spiced beef fills tasty bell pepper halves. Melted cheese topping adds extra goodness!

Large peppers (your favourite), halved lengthwise, seeds and ribs removed	3	3
Boiling water, to cover		
Ice water		
Lean ground beef	1 lb.	454 g
Medium salsa	1 cup	250 mL
Chili powder	1 1/2 tsp.	7 mL
Grated light medium Cheddar cheese	1/2 cup	125 mL
Grated Monterey Jack cheese	1/2 cup	125 mL

Cook pepper halves in boiling water in medium saucepan for about 3 minutes until brightly coloured. Drain. Immediately plunge into ice water in medium bowl. Let stand for about 10 minutes until cold. Drain. Arrange pepper halves, skin-side down, in single layer in ungreased 3 quart (3 L) shallow baking dish.

Scramble-fry ground beef in large non-stick frying pan on medium-high for 5 to 10 minutes until no longer pink. Remove from heat. Drain.

Add salsa and chili powder. Stir well. Divide and spoon beef mixture into each pepper half. Pack lightly.

Combine both cheeses in small bowl. Divide and sprinkle over top of beef mixture. Cook, uncovered, in 350°F (175°C) oven for 20 to 25 minutes until heated through and cheese is melted. Makes 6 stuffed peppers. Serves 6.

1 serving: 222 Calories; 11.9 g Total Fat (4.3 g Mono, 0.5 g Poly, 5.8 g Sat); 53 mg Cholesterol; **9 g Carbohydrate**; 2 g Fibre; 20 g Protein; 282 mg Sodium

Pictured on page 36.

Crisp Minted Salad

A colourful combination of crisp vegetables complements tender strips of beef coated with spicy mint dressing.

Beef rib-eye (or top sirloin) steak, trimmed of fat	1/2 lb.	225 g
Salt	1/4 tsp.	1 mL
Pepper	1/8 tsp.	0.5 mL
Sliced English cucumber (with peel)	1 cup	250 mL
Thinly sliced red pepper	1 cup	250 mL
Fresh bean sprouts (about 3 oz., 86 g)	1 cup	250 mL
Thinly sliced red onion	1/4 cup	60 mL
MINTY LIME DRESSING		
Canola oil	2 tbsp.	30 mL
Lime juice	2 tbsp.	30 mL
Chopped fresh mint leaves (or 1 1/2 tsp., 7 mL, dried)	2 tbsp.	30 mL
Sesame oil, for flavour	1/2 tsp.	2 mL
Chili paste (sambal oelek)	1/2 tsp.	2 mL
Granulated sugar	1/2 tsp.	2 mL
Salt	1/4 tsp.	1 mL

Place steak in shallow baking dish. Sprinkle with salt and pepper. Cover. Chill for 1 hour. Preheat electric grill for 5 minutes or gas barbecue to medium (see Note). Cook steak on greased grill for about 4 minutes per side until desired doneness. Remove from heat. Cover with foil. Let stand for 10 minutes. Cut into thin slices. Transfer to large bowl.

Add next 4 ingredients. Toss.

Minty Lime Dressing: Combine all 7 ingredients in jar with tight-fitting lid. Shake well. Makes about 1/3 cup (75 mL) dressing. Drizzle over salad. Toss. Makes about 4 cups (1 L) salad. Serves 2.

1 serving: 368 Calories; 22.9 g Total Fat (11.9 g Mono, 5 g Poly, 4.2 g Sat); 54 mg Cholesterol; **14 g Carbohydrate**; 3 g Fibre; 28 g Protein; 670 mg Sodium

Pictured on page 36.

Note: Steak may be broiled in oven. Place on greased broiler pan. Broil about 4 inches (10 cm) from heat in oven for about 4 minutes per side until desired doneness.

Simple Pot Roast

Perfect pot roast, served with red wine-flavoured jus infused with rosemary—"jus" delicious!

Canola oil	1 tbsp.	15 mL
Boneless cross-rib (or blade) roast	2 1/2 – 3 lbs.	1.1 – 1.4 kg
Canola oil	1 tbsp.	15 mL
Chopped onion	1 cup	250 mL
Chopped carrot	1 cup	250 mL
Low-sodium prepared beef broth	1 cup	250 mL
Dry red (or alcohol-free) wine	1/2 cup	125 mL
Worcestershire sauce	1 tsp.	5 mL
Dijon mustard (with whole seeds)	1 tsp.	5 mL
Bay leaves	2	2
Salt	1/8 tsp.	0.5 mL
Pepper	1/2 tsp.	2 mL
Sprig of fresh rosemary	1	1

Heat first amount of canola oil in large pot or Dutch oven on medium. Add roast. Cook roast, turning occasionally, until browned on all sides. Remove to large plate. Cover with foil to keep warm.

Heat second amount of canola oil in same pot. Add onion and carrot. Cook for 5 to 10 minutes, stirring often, until onion is softened.

Add next 7 ingredients. Bring to a boil. Return roast to pot. Reduce heat to medium-low. Cover. Simmer for about 2 hours, turning once or twice, until roast is tender. Remove from heat. Transfer roast to large serving plate. Cover with foil. Let stand for 15 minutes. Strain liquid in pot through sieve into medium bowl. Discard solids. Skim and discard fat from surface of liquid with spoon. Return liquid to same pot.

Add rosemary sprig. Bring to a boil on medium. Boil, uncovered, for about 15 minutes until liquid is reduced by half. Remove and discard rosemary sprig. Makes about 1 1/4 cups (300 mL) jus. Serve with roast. Serves 10.

1 serving: 125 Calories; 3.5 g Total Fat (1.4 g Mono, 0.2 g Poly, 1.3 g Sat); 44 mg Cholesterol; **2 g Carbohydrate**; trace Fibre; 18 g Protein; 149 mg Sodium

Beef And Cabbage Wedges

Tender wedges of cabbage topped with seasoned beef and melted cheese. Satisfying.

Lean ground beef	1 lb.	454 g
Chopped onion	1/4 cup	60 mL
Garlic clove, minced (or 1/4 tsp., 1 mL, powder), optional	1	1
Can of diced tomatoes (with juice)	14 oz.	398 mL
Chopped green pepper	1/2 cup	125 mL
Caraway seed	1/2 tsp.	2 mL
Salt	1/4 tsp.	1 mL
Pepper	1/4 tsp.	1 mL
Small head of cabbage (about 1 1/2 – 2 lbs., 680 – 900 g)	1	1
Boiling water	2 cups	500 mL
Salt	1/2 tsp.	2 mL
Grated part-skim mozzarella cheese	1 cup	250 mL

Scramble-fry ground beef, onion and garlic in large non-stick frying pan on medium-high for 5 to 10 minutes until beef is no longer pink and onion is softened. Drain.

Add next 5 ingredients. Stir. Bring to a boil. Reduce heat to medium-low. Simmer, uncovered, for about 15 minutes, stirring occasionally, until liquid is almost evaporated. Cover to keep warm. Set aside.

Cut cabbage into 6 equal wedges. Cut each wedge in half crosswise. Cook, covered, in boiling water and salt in large saucepan for about 10 minutes until tender-crisp. Drain. Arrange cabbage wedges in single layer in greased 1 1/2 quart (1.5 L) shallow baking dish. Spread beef mixture evenly over cabbage.

Sprinkle with cheese. Cook, uncovered, in 350°F (175°C) oven for about 30 minutes until heated through and cheese is melted. Serves 6.

1 serving: 217 Calories; 10.3 g Total Fat (3.8 g Mono, 0.6 g Poly, 4.7 g Sat); 50 mg Cholesterol; **11 g Carbohydrate**; 3 g Fibre; 21 g Protein; 364 mg Sodium

Beef Stir-Fry

A light coating of black bean sauce with a hint of ginger and garlic adds zip to beef and vegetables. A low-carb meal to satisfy.

Low-sodium prepared beef broth	1/4 cup	60 mL
Black bean sauce (pourable)	3 tbsp.	50 mL
Cornstarch	2 tsp.	10 mL
Chili paste (sambal oelek)	1 tsp.	5 mL
Beef top sirloin steak, cut across grain into 1/8 inch (3 mm) thick slices (see Tip, below)	1/2 lb.	225 g
Canola oil	1 tbsp.	15 mL
Canola oil	1 tbsp.	15 mL
Broccoli florets	2 cups	500 mL
Can of sliced water chestnuts, drained	8 oz.	227 mL
Small onion, cut lengthwise into thin wedges	1	1
Garlic clove, minced (or 1/4 tsp., 1 mL, powder)	1	1
Finely grated, peeled gingerroot	1/2 tsp.	2 mL

Combine first 4 ingredients in 1 cup (250 mL) liquid measure. Set aside.

Cut beef slices into 2 inch (5 cm) long strips. Heat wok or large frying pan on medium-high until very hot. Add first amount of canola oil. Add beef. Stir-fry for about 2 minutes until desired doneness. Remove to medium bowl. Set aside.

Heat second amount of canola oil in same wok. Add remaining 5 ingredients. Stir-fry for about 2 minutes until broccoli is tender-crisp. Stir broth mixture. Add to vegetables. Add beef. Stir-fry for about 1 minute until sauce is boiling and thickened. Serves 2.

1 serving: 423 Calories; 26.2 g Total Fat (13.5 g Mono, 5.2 g Poly, 5.2 g Sat); 56 mg Cholesterol; **22 g Carbohydrate**; 5 g Fibre; 27 g Protein; 1168 mg Sodium

To slice meat easily, place in freezer for about 30 minutes until just starting to freeze. If using from frozen state, partially thaw before cutting.

Rosemary Wine Meatloaf

A moist meatloaf subtly flavoured with wine. Just as tasty hot or cold.

Finely chopped onion	2/3 cup	150 mL
Quick-cooking rolled oats (not instant)	1/2 cup	125 mL
Grated light sharp Cheddar cheese	1/2 cup	125 mL
Grated carrot	1/2 cup	125 mL
Large egg, fork-beaten	1	1
Garlic cloves, minced (or 1/2 tsp., 2 mL, powder)	2	2
Chopped fresh rosemary leaves (or 1/4 tsp., 1 mL, dried, crushed)	1 tsp.	5 mL
Celery salt	1/2 tsp.	2 mL
Lean ground beef	1 lb.	454 g
Dry red (or alcohol-free) wine	1/4 cup	60 mL
Tomato paste (see Tip, below) or ketchup	1 tbsp.	15 mL

Combine first 8 ingredients in large bowl.

Add ground beef. Mix well. Press evenly in greased 8 x 4 x 3 inch (20 x 10 x 7.5 cm) loaf pan. Cook, uncovered, in 350°F (175°C) oven for 45 minutes. Remove from oven. Drain.

Combine wine and tomato paste in 1 cup (250 mL) liquid measure. Spread evenly over meatloaf. Cook, uncovered, for about 20 minutes until meatloaf is firm and no longer pink inside. Remove from oven. Cover with foil. Let stand for 10 minutes. Cuts into 8 slices. Serves 4.

1 serving: 323 Calories; 15 g Total Fat (5.9 g Mono, 1 g Poly, 6.3 g Sat); 119 mg Cholesterol; **15 g Carbohydrate**; 2 g Fibre; 28 g Protein; 328 mg Sodium

If a recipe calls for less than an entire can of tomato paste, freeze unopened can for 30 minutes. Open both ends and push contents through one end. Slice off only what you need. Freeze remaining paste in resealable freezer bag or plastic wrap for future use.

Beef And Pea Toss

Sweet curry sauce coats tender strips of beef and bright green pea pods in this tasty dish.

MANGO MARINADE		
Plain yogurt	1/3 cup	75 mL
Mango chutney	3 tbsp.	50 mL
Water	3 tbsp.	50 mL
Curry powder	2 tsp.	10 mL
Beef top sirloin steak, cut across the grain into 1/8 inch (3 mm) thick slices (see Tip, page 43)	1 lb.	454 g
Canola oil	1 tbsp.	15 mL
Low-sodium prepared chicken broth (or water)	1 tbsp.	15 mL
Hard margarine (or butter)	1 tsp.	5 mL
Bag of sugar snap peas, trimmed (about 2 cups, 500 mL)	8 oz.	227 g

Mango Marinade: Combine first 4 ingredients in large bowl. Makes about 3/4 cup (175 mL) marinade.

Cut beef slices into 2 inch (5 cm) long strips. Add to marinade. Stir until coated. Cover. Marinate in refrigerator for 1 to 3 hours.

Heat wok or large frying pan on medium-high until very hot. Add canola oil. Add beef mixture. Stir-fry for 3 to 4 minutes until desired doneness. Remove to separate large bowl. Set aside.

Heat broth and margarine in same wok until margarine is melted. Add peas. Cook for 2 to 3 minutes, stirring occasionally, until peas are bright green. Add beef mixture. Stir-fry until peas are tender-crisp and mixture is heated through. Serves 4.

1 serving: 284 Calories; 15.1 g Total Fat (7.1 g Mono, 1.6 g Poly, 4.7 g Sat); 57 mg Cholesterol; **11 g Carbohydrate**; 2 g Fibre; 24 g Protein; 101 mg Sodium

Spinach Taco Salad

A Tex-Mex-style salad with a crunchy combination of greens and a creamy salsa sauce.

Lean ground beef	1 lb.	454 g
Chopped onion	1/4 cup	60 mL
Chili powder	1 1/2 tsp.	7 mL
Garlic clove, minced (or 1/4 tsp., 1 mL, powder)	1	1
Pepper	1/2 tsp.	2 mL
Chopped or torn iceberg lettuce, lightly packed	4 cups	1 L
Chopped or torn fresh spinach, stems removed, lightly packed	2 cups	500 mL
Diced English cucumber (with peel)	2 cups	500 mL
Chopped red pepper	1 cup	250 mL
Light sour cream	6 tbsp.	100 mL
Salsa	2 1/2 tbsp.	37 mL
Broken up corn tortilla chips	1 cup	250 mL
Grated light medium Cheddar cheese	1 1/2 cups	375 mL

Scramble-fry first 5 ingredients in large non-stick frying pan on medium-high for 5 to 10 minutes until ground beef is no longer pink and onion is softened. Drain. Set aside.

Put next 4 ingredients into large bowl. Toss.

Combine sour cream and salsa in small bowl. Add to lettuce mixture. Toss. Divide and arrange lettuce mixture on 4 individual plates. Divide and spoon beef mixture over each.

Sprinkle tortilla chips and cheese over top of each. Serves 4.

1 serving: 441 Calories; 24.4 g Total Fat (10 g Mono, 1.3 g Poly, 12.2 g Sat); 85 mg Cholesterol; **19 g Carbohydrate**; 3 g Fibre; 36 g Protein; 494 mg Sodium

Pictured on page 36.

Chicken In Flowers

Flavourful, juicy chicken seasoned with garlic and rosemary, surrounded with roasted cauliflower and broccoli. An elegant presentation when you want to carve the chicken at the table.

GARLIC ROSEMARY MARINADE

Garlic cloves, minced (or 1 1/2 tsp., 7 mL, powder)	6	6
Small orange, grated zest and juice	1	1
Finely chopped fresh rosemary leaves (or 3/4 tsp., 4 mL, dried, crushed)	1 tbsp.	15 mL
Canola oil	1 tbsp.	15 mL
Salt	1 tsp.	5 mL
Pepper	1/2 tsp.	2 mL
Whole chicken, rinsed and patted dry	4 lbs.	1.8 kg
Broccoli florets	2 cups	500 mL
Cauliflower florets	2 cups	500 mL
Water	1/4 cup	60 mL

Garlic Rosemary Marinade: Combine first 6 ingredients in small bowl. Makes about 1/3 cup (75 mL) marinade.

Put chicken into large resealable freezer bag. Pour marinade over top. Seal bag. Turn until coated. Marinate in refrigerator for at least 6 hours or overnight, turning occasionally. Drain and discard marinade. Place chicken, breast-side up, on greased wire rack set in small roasting pan. Tie legs together with butcher's string. Tie wings to body. Cover. Cook in 375°F (190°C) oven for about 1 1/2 hours until meat thermometer inserted into thickest part of thigh reads 185°F (85°C). Transfer chicken to large serving dish. Cover with foil. Let stand until ready to serve. Remove and discard butcher's string.

Put broccoli, cauliflower and water into same roasting pan. Stir. Cover. Cook in 375°F (190°C) oven for 15 to 20 minutes until vegetables are tender-crisp. Arrange vegetables around chicken on serving dish. Serves 6.

1 serving: 431 Calories; 29.1 g Total Fat (12.2 g Mono, 6.4 g Poly, 8.1 g Sat); 138 mg Cholesterol; **5 g Carbohydrate**; 2 g Fibre; 36 g Protein; 346 mg Sodium

Chicken Florentine

Thick, tangy tomato sauce surrounds juicy chicken topped with spinach and melted cheese.

Boneless, skinless chicken breast halves (4 – 6 oz., 113 – 170 g, each)	4	4
Salt, sprinkle		
Pepper, sprinkle		
Olive (or canola) oil	1 tbsp.	15 mL
Box of frozen chopped spinach, thawed and squeezed dry	10 oz.	300 g
Deli Gruyère (or Swiss) cheese slices (about 3 oz., 85 g)	4	4
Olive (or canola) oil	1 tbsp.	15 mL
Finely chopped onion	1/3 cup	75 mL
Garlic cloves, minced (or 1/2 tsp., 2 mL, powder)	2	2
Can of crushed tomatoes	14 oz.	398 mL
Dry white (or alcohol-free) wine	1/4 cup	60 mL
Salt	1/4 tsp.	1 mL
Pepper	1/4 tsp.	1 mL

Place 1 chicken breast half between 2 sheets of plastic wrap. Pound with mallet or rolling pin to 1/2 inch (12 mm) thickness. Repeat with remaining chicken breast halves. Sprinkle each with salt and pepper.

Heat first amount of olive oil in large frying pan on medium. Add chicken breast halves. Cook for about 5 minutes per side until no longer pink inside. Remove to large serving dish.

Divide and spoon spinach evenly over each chicken breast half. Press spinach down with back of spoon. Place 1 cheese slice over top of each. Set aside.

Heat second amount of olive oil in same frying pan on medium. Add onion. Cook for 5 to 10 minutes, stirring often, until softened.

Add garlic. Heat and stir for 1 to 2 minutes until fragrant.

Add remaining 4 ingredients. Stir. Bring to a boil. Boil, uncovered, for about 3 minutes until slightly thickened. Reduce heat to medium-low. Carefully place chicken breast halves on top. Cover. Cook for 5 to 10 minutes until heated through and cheese slices are melted. Serves 4.

1 serving: 358 Calories; 16.6 g Total Fat (6.8 g Mono, 3.2 g Poly, 5.2 g Sat); 105 mg Cholesterol; **9 g Carbohydrate**; 3 g Fibre; 41 g Protein; 432 mg Sodium

Chicken Kabobs

Delicate dill and tangy tomato add a fresh, light flavour to grilled chicken.

Balsamic vinegar	3 tbsp.	50 mL
Chopped fresh dill (or 1 1/2 tsp., 7 mL, dill weed)	2 tbsp.	30 mL
Dijon mustard	2 tsp.	10 mL
Salt	1/8 tsp.	0.5 mL
Pepper	1/4 tsp.	1 mL
Boneless, skinless chicken thighs, cut into 1 inch (2.5 cm) pieces	1 lb.	454 g
Small zucchini (with peel), cut into 1/2 inch (12 mm) slices	2	2
Cherry tomatoes	24	24
Bamboo skewers (8 inch, 20 cm, length), soaked in water for 10 minutes	8	8

Combine first 5 ingredients in small bowl.

Thread chicken pieces, zucchini slices and tomatoes alternately onto skewers. Brush with vinegar mixture. Preheat electric grill for 5 minutes or gas barbecue to medium (see Note). Cook kabobs on greased grill for about 15 minutes, turning occasionally, brushing with remaining vinegar mixture, until chicken is no longer pink inside and zucchini is tender-crisp. Makes 8 kabobs. Serves 4.

1 serving: 182 Calories; 6.7 g Total Fat (2 g Mono, 2.2 g Poly, 1.6 g Sat); 94 mg Cholesterol; **7 g Carbohydrate**; 2 g Fibre; 24 g Protein; 127 mg Sodium

Pictured on front cover.

Note: Kabobs may be broiled in oven. Place on greased broiler pan. Broil about 4 inches (10 cm) from heat in oven for about 15 minutes, turning occasionally, brushing with remaining vinegar mixture, until chicken is no longer pink inside and zucchini is tender-crisp.

Chicken And Spinach

Tender chicken on tangy creamed spinach. Colourful and appetizing.

Boneless, skinless chicken breast halves (4 – 6 oz., 113 – 170 g, each)	4	4
Large egg, fork-beaten	1	1
Hard margarine (or butter)	2 tbsp.	30 mL
Canola oil	1 tsp.	5 mL
Chopped red pepper	1/2 cup	125 mL
Chopped onion	2 tbsp.	30 mL
Box of frozen chopped spinach, thawed and squeezed dry	10 oz.	300 g
Seasoned salt	1 tsp.	5 mL
Light (or regular) sour cream	1/2 cup	125 mL

Dip each chicken breast half into egg in small shallow dish until coated.

Melt margarine in large frying pan on medium. Add chicken breast halves. Cook for about 2 minutes per side until lightly browned. Transfer to greased 1 quart (1 L) shallow baking dish. Cook, uncovered, in 350°F (175°C) oven for about 10 minutes until chicken is no longer pink inside. Transfer to medium serving dish. Cover to keep warm.

Heat canola oil in same frying pan on medium. Add red pepper and onion. Cook for 5 to 10 minutes, stirring often, until onion is softened.

Add spinach and seasoned salt. Heat and stir for about 3 minutes until heated through.

Add sour cream. Stir. Divide and spoon spinach mixture onto each of 4 individual plates. Cut each chicken breast half into 5 slices. Place 1 sliced chicken breast half on top of spinach mixture on each plate. Serves 4.

1 serving: 286 Calories; 13 g Total Fat (6.7 g Mono, 1.9 g Poly, 5 g Sat); 141 mg Cholesterol; **6 g Carbohydrate**; 2 g Fibre; 36 g Protein; 440 mg Sodium

Pictured on page 53.

Turkey Patties

Ground turkey patties seasoned with basil and topped with an enticing pesto mayonnaise and fresh vegetables. Great for a light supper.

Finely chopped fresh basil (or 2 1/4 tsp., 11 mL, dried)	3 tbsp.	50 mL
Fresh (or fine dry) bread crumbs	2 tbsp.	30 mL
Large egg, fork-beaten	1	1
Low-sodium soy sauce	1 tbsp.	15 mL
Italian seasoning	1 tsp.	5 mL
Lean ground turkey	1 lb.	454 g
PESTO MAYONNAISE		
Low-fat mayonnaise	1/4 cup	60 mL
Sun-dried tomato pesto	2 tbsp.	30 mL
Red onion slices (about 1/4 inch, 6 mm, thick)	4	4
Mixed salad greens	1 cup	250 mL
Tomato slices (about 1/4 inch, 6 mm, thick)	4	4

Combine first 5 ingredients in medium bowl.

Add ground turkey. Mix well. Divide into 4 equal portions. Shape each portion into 4 1/2 inch (11 cm) diameter patty. Place patties on greased broiler pan. Broil about 4 inches (10 cm) from heat in oven for about 4 minutes per side until no longer pink inside. Transfer to medium serving dish. Cover to keep warm.

Pesto Mayonnaise: Combine mayonnaise and pesto in small bowl. Makes about 1/3 cup (75 mL) mayonnaise.

Spread mayonnaise evenly on 1 side of each patty. Divide and layer onion slices, salad greens and tomato slices, in order given, on top of mayonnaise. Serves 4.

1 serving: 278 Calories; 17.1 g Total Fat (7.7 g Mono, 4.4 g Poly, 3.4 g Sat); 144 mg Cholesterol; **8 g Carbohydrate**; 1 g Fibre; 23 g Protein; 414 mg Sodium

Pictured on front cover.

Almond Cheese Chicken

Attractive, golden chicken will have everyone eager to eat! A great dish for company.

Boneless, skinless chicken breast halves **(4 – 6 oz., 113 – 170 g, each)**	**4**	**4**
Ground almonds	**1 cup**	**250 mL**
Grated Parmesan cheese	**2/3 cup**	**150 mL**
Salt	**1/4 tsp.**	**1 mL**
Pepper	**1/4 tsp.**	**1 mL**
All-purpose flour	**2 tbsp.**	**30 mL**
Large eggs, fork-beaten	**2**	**2**

Place 1 chicken breast half between 2 sheets of plastic wrap. Pound with mallet or rolling pin to 1/2 inch (12 mm) thickness. Repeat with remaining chicken breast halves.

Combine next 4 ingredients in small shallow dish.

Dredge each chicken breast half in flour in separate small shallow dish. Dip into egg in small bowl. Press both sides of each chicken breast half into almond mixture until coated. Arrange chicken in single layer on greased foil-lined baking sheet with sides. Cook, uncovered, in 350°F (175°C) oven for about 45 minutes until no longer pink inside. Serves 4.

1 serving: 390 Calories; 19.1 g Total Fat (8.8 g Mono, 2.9 g Poly, 5.6 g Sat); 203 mg Cholesterol; **8 g Carbohydrate**; trace Fibre; 46 g Protein; 509 mg Sodium

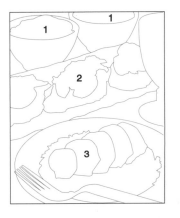

1. Spicy Balsamic Chicken, page 56
2. Crumbed Chicken Melt, page 58
3. Chicken And Spinach, page 50

Roasted Chicken

Herb and butter combination makes chicken moist and juicy. Bacon adds a satisfying, smoky surprise.

Butter (or hard margarine), softened	3 tbsp.	50 mL
Bacon slices, cooked crisp and crumbled	2	2
Finely chopped fresh thyme leaves (or 1/2 tsp., 2 mL, dried)	2 tsp.	10 mL
Celery salt	1/4 tsp.	1 mL
Pepper	1/4 tsp.	1 mL
Whole chicken, rinsed and patted dry	3 lbs.	1.4 kg
Butter (or hard margarine), softened	1 tsp.	5 mL

Combine first 5 ingredients in small bowl.

Loosen skin of chicken breast and thighs. Spread butter mixture evenly between flesh and skin of chicken with soft spatula, being careful not to pierce skin. Tie legs together with butcher's string. Tie wings to body.

Rub second amount of butter evenly over skin of chicken. Place chicken, breast-side up, on greased wire rack set in small roasting pan. Cover. Cook in 350°F (175°C) oven for 1 1/4 to 1 1/2 hours until meat thermometer inserted into thickest part of thigh reads 185°F (85°C). Remove from oven. Let stand, covered, for 10 minutes. Remove and discard butcher's string. Serves 4.

1 serving: 424 Calories; 29.5 g Total Fat (10.7 g Mono, 4.5 g Poly, 11.7 g Sat); 147 mg Cholesterol; **0 g Carbohydrate**; trace Fibre; 38 g Protein; 337 mg Sodium

1. Shrimp And Asparagus, page 63
2. Nut-Crusted Sole, page 68
3. Fish Cakes, page 66

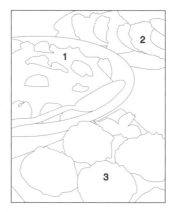

Spicy Balsamic Chicken

Fragrant, with a hint of sweetness. Sure to be a hit!

Canola oil	1 tbsp.	15 mL
Boneless, skinless chicken breast halves, thinly sliced across grain (see Tip, page 43)	1/2 lb.	225 g
Thinly sliced red pepper	1 cup	250 mL
Red onion, cut into thin wedges	1/2	1/2
Sweet chili sauce	1 tbsp.	15 mL
Finely shredded fresh basil (or 3/4 tsp., 4 mL, dried)	1 tbsp.	15 mL
Garlic cloves, minced (or 1/2 tsp., 2 mL, powder)	2	2
Balsamic vinegar	2 tsp.	10 mL
Chili paste (sambal oelek)	1/2 – 1 tsp.	2 – 5 mL
Salt, sprinkle		
Pepper, sprinkle		

Heat wok or large frying pan on medium-high until very hot. Add canola oil. Add chicken slices. Stir-fry for about 3 minutes until almost cooked.

Add remaining 9 ingredients. Stir-fry for about 3 minutes until chicken is no longer pink and red pepper is tender-crisp. Serves 2.

1 serving: 264 Calories; 9.5 g Total Fat (4.7 g Mono, 2.7 g Poly, 1.2 g Sat); 81 mg Cholesterol; **11 g Carbohydrate**; 2 g Fibre; 33 g Protein; 119 mg Sodium

Pictured on page 53.

Cajun Roast Chicken

Add a little pep to your poultry with this zippy Cajun coating.

Canola oil	2 tbsp.	30 mL
Paprika	1 tbsp.	15 mL
Dried whole oregano	1 1/2 tsp.	7 mL
Dried thyme	1 1/2 tsp.	7 mL
Salt	1 tsp.	5 mL
Garlic powder	1/2 tsp.	2 mL
Cayenne pepper	1/4 tsp.	1 mL
Medium onion, cut in half	1	1
Whole chicken, rinsed and patted dry	4 lbs.	1.8 kg

(continued on next page)

Combine first 7 ingredients in small cup.

Place onion halves inside chicken. Rub spice mixture evenly over skin of chicken. Tie legs together with butcher's string. Tie wings to body. Place chicken, breast-side up, on greased wire rack set in small roasting pan. Cover. Cook in 375°F (190°C) oven for about 1 1/2 hours until meat thermometer inserted into thickest part of thigh reads 185°F (85°C). Remove from oven. Let stand, covered, for 10 minutes. Remove and discard butcher's string and onion halves. Serves 6.

1 serving: 331 Calories; 21 g Total Fat (9.1 g Mono, 5 g Poly, 4.9 g Sat); 105 mg Cholesterol; **1 g Carbohydrate**; trace Fibre; 33 g Protein; 494 mg Sodium

Marinated Herb Chicken

White wine adds a touch of elegance to this simple but delicious dish.

HERB MARINADE

Dry white (or alcohol-free) wine	**1/4 cup**	**60 mL**
Chopped green onion	**1/4 cup**	**60 mL**
Olive (or canola) oil	**3 tbsp.**	**50 mL**
Chopped fresh basil (or 1 1/2 tsp., 7 mL, dried)	**2 tbsp.**	**30 mL**
Chopped fresh parsley (or 1 1/2 tsp., 7 mL, flakes)	**2 tbsp.**	**30 mL**
Garlic cloves, minced (or 1/2 tsp., 2 mL, powder)	**2**	**2**
Salt	**1/4 tsp.**	**1 mL**
Pepper	**1/4 tsp.**	**1 mL**
Boneless, skinless chicken breast halves (4 – 6 oz., 113 – 170 g, each)	**4**	**4**

Herb Marinade: Combine first 8 ingredients in small bowl. Makes about 1/2 cup (125 mL) marinade.

Put chicken breast halves into large resealable freezer bag. Pour marinade over top. Seal bag. Turn until coated. Marinate in refrigerator for at least 6 hours or overnight, turning occasionally. Drain and discard marinade. Preheat electric grill for 5 minutes or gas barbecue to medium (see Note). Cook chicken breast halves on greased grill for 8 to 10 minutes per side until no longer pink inside. Serves 4.

1 serving: 209 Calories; 7.6 g Total Fat (3.6 g Mono, 2.1 g Poly, 1 g Sat); 81 mg Cholesterol; **1 g Carbohydrate**; trace Fibre; 32 g Protein; 79 mg Sodium

Note: Chicken may be broiled in oven. Place on greased broiler pan. Broil about 4 inches (10 cm) from heat in oven for 8 to 10 minutes per side until no longer pink inside.

Crumbed Chicken Melt

Crunchy crumb-coated chicken topped with buttery avocado, tangy tomato, red pepper and melted cheese. A whole meal in one pretty presentation!

Boneless, skinless chicken breast halves (4 – 6 oz., 113 – 170 g, each)	**4**	**4**
Large eggs, fork-beaten	**1**	**1**
Cornflake crumbs	**3/4 cup**	**175 mL**
Ripe large avocado, sliced	**1**	**1**
Finely chopped tomato	**1/3 cup**	**75 mL**
Finely chopped red (or yellow) pepper	**1/3 cup**	**75 mL**
Pepper, sprinkle		
Grated Parmesan (or Asiago) cheese	**2/3 cup**	**150 mL**

Place 1 chicken breast half between 2 sheets of plastic wrap. Pound with mallet or rolling pin to 1/2 inch (12 mm) thickness. Repeat with remaining chicken breast halves.

Dip each chicken breast half into egg in small bowl. Press both sides of each chicken breast half into cornflake crumbs in small shallow dish until coated. Arrange chicken in single layer on greased foil-lined baking sheet with sides. Cook, uncovered, in 350°F (175°C) oven for about 45 minutes until no longer pink inside.

Top each chicken breast half with next 5 ingredients in order given. Broil about 4 inches (10 cm) from heat in oven for 2 to 3 minutes until cheese is melted and golden. Serves 4.

1 serving: 414 Calories; 16.7 g Total Fat (7.4 g Mono, 1.8 g Poly, 5.6 g Sat); 149 mg Cholesterol; **22 g Carbohydrate**; 2 g Fibre; 43 g Protein; 534 mg Sodium

Pictured on page 53.

Curry Chicken Drumettes

Sweet, creamy curry dip makes these golden drumettes even more enjoyable. Part of a light dinner.

PLUM MARINADE		
Plum sauce	1/2 cup	125 mL
Water	1/4 cup	60 mL
Curry powder	2 tbsp.	30 mL
Worcestershire sauce	1 1/2 tbsp.	25 mL
Pepper	1 tsp.	5 mL
Chicken drumettes (about 24), skin removed, or whole chicken wings, split in half and tips discarded (about 36 pieces), skin removed	3 lbs.	1.4 kg

CREAMY CURRY DIP		
Light sour cream	1/2 cup	125 mL
Low-fat mayonnaise	2 tbsp.	30 mL
Plum sauce	2 tbsp.	30 mL
Curry powder	2 tsp.	10 mL

Plum Marinade: Combine first 5 ingredients in small bowl. Makes about 1 cup (250 mL) marinade.

Put drumettes into large resealable freezer bag. Pour marinade over top. Seal bag. Turn until coated. Marinate in refrigerator for at least 6 hours or overnight, turning occasionally. Drain and discard marinade. Arrange drumettes in single layer on greased foil-lined baking sheet with sides. Cook, uncovered, in 350°F (175°C) oven for about 45 minutes, turning occasionally, until chicken is no longer pink inside.

Creamy Curry Dip: Combine all 4 ingredients in small bowl. Makes about 3/4 cup (175 mL) dip. Serve with drumettes. Serves 4.

1 serving: 346 Calories; 15.1 g Total Fat (5.9 g Mono, 3.1 g Poly, 5.7 g Sat); 113 mg Cholesterol; **11 g Carbohydrate**; 1 g Fibre; 40 g Protein; 292 mg Sodium

Red Curry Chicken

Slightly sweet curry and coconut sauce with an enjoyable, mild heat generously coats chicken and asparagus. Serve with sliced cucumber, tomato and red onion.

Water	**1 tbsp.**	**15 mL**
Cornstarch	**1 1/2 tsp.**	**7 mL**
Canola oil	**1 tbsp.**	**15 mL**
Boneless, skinless chicken breast halves, thinly sliced (see Tip, page 43)	**1 1/2 lbs.**	**680 g**
Red curry paste	**1 tbsp.**	**15 mL**
Can of coconut milk	**14 oz.**	**398 mL**
Lime juice	**1 tbsp.**	**15 mL**
Liquid honey	**2 tsp.**	**10 mL**
Fish sauce	**1 tsp.**	**5 mL**
Fresh asparagus, trimmed of tough ends, cut into 1 inch (2.5 cm) pieces	**1 lb.**	**454 g**
Chopped fresh cilantro or parsley (or 1 1/2 tsp., 7 mL, dried)	**2 tbsp.**	**30 mL**

Stir water into cornstarch in small cup until smooth. Set aside.

Heat wok or large frying pan on medium-high until very hot. Add canola oil. Add chicken slices. Stir-fry for about 5 minutes until no longer pink.

Add curry paste. Heat and stir for about 1 minute until fragrant.

Add next 4 ingredients. Stir. Bring to a boil. Boil, uncovered, for 10 to 15 minutes, stirring occasionally, until sauce is slightly reduced.

Add asparagus and cilantro. Stir. Cook, uncovered, for about 3 minutes, stirring occasionally, until asparagus is tender-crisp. Stir cornstarch mixture. Add to chicken mixture. Heat and stir until sauce is boiling and thickened. Serves 6.

1 serving: 294 Calories; 19.2 g Total Fat (3.2 g Mono, 1.7 g Poly, 12.7 g Sat); 54 mg Cholesterol; **9 g Carbohydrate**; 1 g Fibre; 24 g Protein; 69 mg Sodium

Shrimp And Sprouts

A crisp, showy salad. Add more chili paste if you prefer a spicier dressing.

ASIAN DRESSING		
Granulated sugar	1 tsp.	5 mL
Chili paste (sambal oelek)	1/2 tsp.	2 mL
Garlic clove, minced (or 1/4 tsp., 1 mL, powder)	1	1
Pepper, sprinkle		
Canola oil	1/4 cup	60 mL
Lime (or lemon) juice	2 tbsp.	30 mL
Fish sauce	2 tbsp.	30 mL
Finely shredded red cabbage, lightly packed	2 cups	500 mL
Finely shredded green cabbage, lightly packed	2 cups	500 mL
Fresh bean sprouts (about 4 oz., 113 g)	1 1/2 cups	375 mL
Small cooked shrimp (about 6 oz., 170 g)	1 1/4 cups	300 mL
Julienned English cucumber (with peel), see Note	1 cup	250 mL
Green onions, cut crosswise into 3 inch (7.5 cm) pieces, then cut lengthwise into very thin slivers	2	2
Small carrot, thinly sliced diagonally	1	1
Celery rib, thinly sliced diagonally	1	1
Chopped salted peanuts	1/4 cup	60 mL

Asian Dressing: Combine first 7 ingredients in small bowl. Let stand for 15 minutes to blend flavours. Makes about 1/2 cup (125 mL) dressing.

Put next 8 ingredients into large bowl. Toss gently. Drizzle dressing over top. Toss gently.

Scatter peanuts over top. Makes about 8 1/2 cups (2.1 L) salad. Serves 6.

1 serving: 201 Calories; 13.7 g Total Fat (7.4 g Mono, 4.2 g Poly, 1.3 g Sat); 49 mg Cholesterol; **11 g Carbohydrate**; 3 g Fibre; 11 g Protein; 472 mg Sodium

Pictured on page 72.

Note: To cut vegetables julienne, cut into 1/8 inch (3 mm) strips that resemble matchsticks.

Variation: Omit shrimp. Use same amount of diced cooked chicken or ham.

Salmon Soufflé

Turn simple canned salmon into a spectacular, lightly seasoned soufflé everyone will love!

Ingredient	Imperial	Metric
Hard margarine (or butter), softened	1 tsp.	5 mL
Fine dry bread crumbs	2 tbsp.	30 mL
Hard margarine (or butter)	2 tbsp.	30 mL
All-purpose flour	1/4 cup	60 mL
Milk	1 1/2 cups	375 mL
Dijon mustard	2 tsp.	10 mL
Salt	1/4 tsp.	1 mL
Pepper	1/4 tsp.	1 mL
Cans of red salmon (7 1/2 oz., 213 g, each), drained, skin and round bones removed, flaked	2	2
Egg yolks (large), fork-beaten	4	4
Chopped fresh dill (or 3/4 tsp., 4 mL, dill weed)	1 tbsp.	15 mL
Egg whites (large)	4	4

Preheat oven to 375°F (190°C). Grease 6 cup (1.6 L) soufflé dish (round casserole with high, straight side) with first amount of margarine. Sprinkle with bread crumbs. Turn dish to coat bottom and side. Gently tap dish to remove excess bread crumbs. Set aside.

Melt second amount of margarine in medium saucepan on medium. Add flour. Heat and stir for 1 minute.

Slowly add milk, stirring constantly, until smooth. Add mustard, salt and pepper. Heat and stir for about 5 minutes until boiling and thickened. Cool.

Add next 3 ingredients to milk mixture. Mix well.

Beat egg whites in medium bowl until stiff peaks form. Carefully fold about 1/3 of egg white into salmon mixture until almost combined. Fold in remaining egg white until just combined. Carefully spoon salmon mixture into prepared soufflé dish. Spread evenly. Bake for about 45 minutes, without opening oven door, until puffed and set. Serve immediately. Serves 4.

1 serving: 385 Calories; 23.4 g Total Fat (11.1 g Mono, 4.5 g Poly, 6 g Sat); 244 mg Cholesterol; **14 g Carbohydrate**; trace Fibre; 28 g Protein; 823 mg Sodium

Shrimp And Asparagus

Bright green vegetables show off pretty pink shrimp—all coated in a smooth, buttery orange sauce.

Ingredient	Imperial	Metric
Butter (or hard margarine)	2 tbsp.	30 mL
Orange juice	1/3 cup	75 mL
Chopped green onion	1/3 cup	75 mL
Grated orange zest	1 tsp.	5 mL
Salt	1/4 tsp.	1 mL
Pepper	1/4 tsp.	1 mL
Fresh asparagus, trimmed of tough ends, halved	1 lb.	454 g
Snow peas, trimmed	9 oz.	255 g
Fresh uncooked medium shrimp, peeled and deveined	12 oz.	340 g
Water	1 tbsp.	15 mL
Cornstarch	1 tsp.	5 mL

Melt butter in large frying pan on medium. Add next 5 ingredients. Heat and stir for 1 to 2 minutes until fragrant.

Add asparagus and peas. Heat and stir for 2 to 4 minutes until vegetables are bright green.

Add shrimp. Cook for about 5 minutes, stirring occasionally, until shrimp are pink and vegetables are tender-crisp.

Stir water into cornstarch in small cup until smooth. Add to shrimp mixture. Heat and stir for about 1 minute until sauce is slightly thickened. Serves 4.

1 serving: 185 Calories; 7.3 g Total Fat (1.9 g Mono, 0.8 g Poly, 3.9 g Sat); 113 mg Cholesterol; **14 g Carbohydrate**; 3 g Fibre; 17 g Protein; 308 mg Sodium

Pictured on page 54.

Pepper Lime Cod

Tender, flaky fish drizzled with zesty lime and sweet chili sauce.

Salt	1/4 tsp.	1 mL
Coarse ground pepper	1 tsp.	5 mL
Cod fillets, cut into 4 equal portions	1 lb.	454 g
Canola oil	1 tbsp.	15 mL
Canola oil	2 tsp.	10 mL
Thinly sliced green onion	3 tbsp.	50 mL
Garlic cloves, minced (or 1/2 tsp., 2 mL, powder)	2	2
Lime juice	1 tbsp.	15 mL
Grated lime zest	1/4 tsp.	1 mL
Sweet chili sauce	1 tbsp.	15 mL
Hard margarine (or butter), softened	2 tbsp.	30 mL

Divide and sprinkle salt and pepper evenly over each cod portion. Heat first amount of canola oil in large frying pan on medium. Add fish. Cook for 3 to 4 minutes per side until fish flakes easily when tested with fork. Remove to large serving dish. Cover to keep warm.

Heat second amount of canola oil in same frying pan. Add onion. Cook for 2 to 3 minutes, stirring often, until softened.

Add garlic. Heat and stir for 1 to 2 minutes until fragrant.

Add lime juice, zest and chili sauce. Stir.

Add margarine. Stir until margarine is melted. Drizzle over fish. Serves 4.

1 serving: 206 Calories; 12.4 g Total Fat (7.3 g Mono, 2.6 g Poly, 1.8 g Sat); 49 mg Cholesterol; **3 g Carbohydrate**; 1 g Fibre; 21 g Protein; 337 mg Sodium

Crab Salad

Crisp vegetables and tender crab coated with smooth, creamy dressing—makes a satisfying meal.

Mixed salad greens, lightly packed	6 cups	1.5 L
Fresh bean sprouts (about 3 oz., 85 g)	1 cup	250 mL
Thinly sliced celery	1/2 cup	125 mL
Sliced fresh white mushrooms	1/2 cup	125 mL
Sliced blanched almonds, toasted (see Tip, page 24)	1/3 cup	75 mL
Green onions, chopped	2	2

(continued on next page)

SOY SAUCE DRESSING

Low-fat salad dressing (or mayonnaise)	1/2 cup	125 mL
Water	3 tbsp.	50 mL
Indonesian sweet (or thick) soy sauce	2 tbsp.	30 mL
White vinegar	1 tsp.	5 mL
Brown sugar, packed	1 tsp.	5 mL
Hot pepper sauce	1/2 tsp.	2 mL
Cans of crabmeat (4 1/4 oz., 120 g, each), drained, cartilage removed, flaked	2	2

Put first 6 ingredients into large bowl. Toss.

Soy Sauce Dressing: Combine first 6 ingredients in small bowl. Makes about 1/2 cup (125 mL) dressing. Drizzle over salad greens mixture. Toss.

Sprinkle crabmeat over top. Makes about 8 cups (2 L) salad. Serves 4.

1 serving: 221 Calories; 13.6 g Total Fat (7.7 g Mono, 3.5 g Poly, 0.9 g Sat); 0 mg Cholesterol; **14 g Carbohydrate**; 3 g Fibre; 13 g Protein; 1161 mg Sodium

Pesto Halibut

Mild pesto flavour adds zing to tasty, flaky fish. Quick and easy to prepare.

BASIL PESTO MAYONNAISE

Low-fat mayonnaise	1/4 cup	60 mL
Basil pesto	2 tbsp.	30 mL
Lemon juice	2 tbsp.	30 mL
Grated lemon zest	1/2 tsp.	2 mL
Salt	1/4 tsp.	1 mL
Pepper	1/8 tsp.	0.5 mL
Halibut fillets (about 4 oz., 113 g, each)	4	4

Basil Pesto Mayonnaise: Combine first 6 ingredients in small bowl. Makes about 1/2 cup (125 mL) pesto mayonnaise.

Preheat two-sided grill for 5 minutes (see Note). Divide and spread mayonnaise evenly on both sides of each halibut fillet. Place fillets on greased grill. Close lid. Cook for about 5 minutes until fish flakes easily when tested with fork. Serves 4.

1 serving: 196 Calories; 9.7 g Total Fat (5 g Mono, 3.1 g Poly, 0.9 g Sat); 36 mg Cholesterol; **2 g Carbohydrate**; trace Fibre; 24 g Protein; 314 mg Sodium

Note: Fish may be broiled in oven. Place on greased broiler pan. Broil about 4 inches (10 cm) from heat in oven for about 5 minutes per side until fish flakes easily when tested with fork.

Fish Cakes

A great dish for dinner! Be sure to remove all bones from the cod.

Cod fillets, bones removed, chopped	1 lb.	454 g
Fresh whole wheat bread crumbs	1/3 cup	75 mL
Chopped green onion	1/4 cup	60 mL
Chopped fresh cilantro or parsley (or 1 1/2 tsp., 7 mL, dried)	2 tbsp.	30 mL
Large egg	1	1
Fish sauce	2 tsp.	10 mL
Garlic cloves, minced (or 1/2 tsp., 2 mL, powder)	2	2
Finely grated, peeled gingerroot	1 tsp.	5 mL
Dried crushed chilies	1 tsp.	5 mL
Cornstarch, approximately	3 tbsp.	50 mL
Canola oil	3 tbsp.	50 mL

Process first 9 ingredients in blender or food processor until almost smooth. Transfer to medium bowl. Divide cod mixture into 12 equal portions. Shape each portion into 1/2 inch (12 mm) thick patty. Patties will be quite delicate.

Sprinkle about 1 1/2 tbsp. (25 mL) cornstarch onto sheet of waxed paper. Place patties in single layer on top of cornstarch. Sprinkle about 1 1/2 tbsp. (25 mL) cornstarch over top of patties until lightly coated.

Heat canola oil in large frying pan on medium. Add patties. Cook for about 3 minutes per side until golden brown. Remove to paper towels to drain. Makes 12 fish cakes. Serves 4.

1 serving: 273 Calories; 13.1 g Total Fat (6.9 g Mono, 3.7 g Poly, 1.4 g Sat); 103 mg Cholesterol; **14 g Carbohydrate**; 1 g Fibre; 24 g Protein; 342 mg Sodium

Pictured on page 54.

Stuffed Rainbow Trout

An attractive way to serve fish. Sweet crab stuffing complements the mild trout flavour.

Salt	1/2 tsp.	2 mL
Whole rainbow trout (7 – 8 oz., 200 – 225 g, each), pan ready	4	4
Can of crabmeat, drained, cartilage removed	4 1/4 oz.	120 g
Low-fat mayonnaise	2 tbsp.	30 mL
Fine dry bread crumbs	2 tbsp.	30 mL
Sweet (or regular) chili sauce	2 tsp.	10 mL
Lemon juice	2 tsp.	10 mL
Canola oil	2 tbsp.	30 mL

Sprinkle salt evenly over flesh side of each fish.

Measure next 5 ingredients into small bowl. Mix well. Divide and spoon crab mixture into each fish. Spread evenly. Tie each fish with butcher's string or secure with metal skewers to enclose filling.

Brush canola oil over skin of each fish. Preheat two-sided grill for 5 minutes (see Note). Arrange fish in single layer on uncreased grill. Close lid. Cook for about 10 minutes until fish flakes easily when tested with fork. Serves 4.

1 serving: 241 Calories; 14.3 g Total Fat (6.8 g Mono, 4.4 g Poly, 2 g Sat); 51 mg Cholesterol; **4 g Carbohydrate**; trace Fibre; 23 g Protein; 639 mg Sodium

Note: Fish may be broiled in oven. Place on greased broiler pan. Broil about 4 inches (10 cm) from heat in oven for about 10 minutes per side until fish flakes easily when tested with fork.

Nut-Crusted Sole

Crunchy nuts and fresh dill are good for the sole—colourful and delicious.

Ground pecans, toasted (see Tip, page 24)	1/3 cup	75 mL
Ground walnuts, toasted (see Tip, page 24)	1/4 cup	60 mL
Ground almonds, toasted (see Tip, page 24)	1/4 cup	60 mL
Chopped fresh dill (or 1 1/2 tsp., 7 mL, dill weed)	2 tbsp.	30 mL
Chopped fresh parsley (or 1 1/4 tsp., 6 mL, flakes)	1 1/2 tbsp.	25 mL
Garlic powder	1 tsp.	5 mL
Paprika	1 tsp.	5 mL
Salt (optional)	1/4 tsp.	1 mL
Sole fillets	1 1/2 lbs.	680 g
Lemon wedges, for garnish	6	6

Combine first 8 ingredients in shallow medium baking dish.

Press both sides of each fillet into nut mixture until coated. Arrange in single layer on greased baking sheet with sides. Cook, uncovered, in 375°F (190°C) oven for 10 to 15 minutes until fish flakes easily when tested with fork. Transfer to serving plate.

Garnish with lemon wedges. Serves 6.

1 serving: 176 Calories; 7.9 g Total Fat (3.5 g Mono, 2.8 g Poly, 0.9 g Sat); 54 mg Cholesterol; **3 g Carbohydrate**; trace Fibre; 23 g Protein; 93 mg Sodium

Pictured on page 54.

Marinated Salmon

The appetizing appearance of this salmon and the sweet ginger accent are sure to make everyone eager to try it!

SHERRY MARINADE

Olive (or canola) oil	1/4 cup	60 mL
Dry sherry	1/4 cup	60 mL
Chopped fresh parsley (or 1 tbsp., 15 mL, flakes)	1/4 cup	60 mL
Low-sodium soy sauce	1 tbsp.	15 mL
Brown sugar, packed	1 tbsp.	15 mL
Finely grated, peeled gingerroot (or 3/4 tsp., 4 mL, ground ginger)	1 tbsp.	15 mL

(continued on next page)

| Salmon fillets (about 1 lb., 454 g), skin removed | 4 | 4 |

Sherry Marinade: Combine first 6 ingredients in small bowl. Makes about 1/2 cup (125 mL) marinade.

Place salmon fillets in large shallow baking dish. Pour marinade over top. Turn until coated. Cover. Marinate in refrigerator for 30 minutes, turning occasionally. Drain and discard marinade. Heat large non-stick frying pan on medium. Add salmon. Cook for about 3 minutes per side until fish flakes easily when tested with fork. Serves 4.

1 serving: 364 Calories; 26.7 g Total Fat (15 g Mono, 5.7 g Poly, 4.4 g Sat); 67 mg Cholesterol; **4 g Carbohydrate**; trace Fibre; 23 g Protein; 194 mg Sodium

Shrimp And Snow Peas

Colourful snow peas, red onion and shrimp in a delicately spiced sauce.

Low-sodium prepared chicken broth	1/2 cup	125 mL
Hoisin sauce	2 tbsp.	30 mL
Teriyaki sauce	1 tbsp.	15 mL
Cornstarch	2 tsp.	10 mL
Canola oil	1 tbsp.	15 mL
Red medium onion, cut into thin wedges (about 1 cup, 250 mL)	1/2	1/2
Garlic cloves, minced (or 1/2 tsp., 2 mL, powder)	2	2
Finely grated, peeled gingerroot	1/2 tsp.	2 mL
Fresh uncooked (or frozen uncooked, thawed) medium shrimp, tails removed, peeled and deveined	1 lb.	454 g
Snow peas, trimmed	2 cups	500 mL

Combine first 4 ingredients in small cup. Set aside.

Heat wok or large frying pan on medium-high until very hot. Add canola oil. Add onion, garlic and ginger. Stir-fry for 2 to 3 minutes until onion is tender-crisp.

Add shrimp and peas. Stir-fry for about 3 minutes until shrimp are pink. Do not overcook. Stir broth mixture. Add to shrimp mixture. Stir-fry for 1 to 2 minutes until peas are tender-crisp and sauce is thickened. Serves 4.

1 serving: 193 Calories; 5.2 g Total Fat (2.3 g Mono, 1.7 g Poly, 0.6 g Sat); 129 mg Cholesterol; **15 g Carbohydrate**; 2 g Fibre; 21 g Protein; 586 mg Sodium

Ginger Lamb Chops

Flavourful seasoned butter melts over grilled lamb chops to add a rich taste to every bite.
Very simple to prepare.

Butter (or hard margarine), softened	2 tbsp.	30 mL
Apricot jam	1 1/2 tsp.	7 mL
Finely grated, peeled gingerroot	1/2 tsp.	2 mL
Dried crushed chilies	1/4 tsp.	1 mL
Salt	1/8 tsp.	0.5 mL
Lamb loin chops (1 1/4 – 1 1/2 lbs., 560 – 680 g)	8	8

Combine first 5 ingredients in small bowl. Cover. Set aside.

Preheat electric grill for 5 minutes or gas barbecue to medium (see Note). Cook lamb chops on greased grill for 4 to 5 minutes per side until desired doneness. Place 2 lamb chops on each of 4 individual plates. Spoon 1 tsp. (5 mL) butter mixture on top of each lamb chop. Serves 4.

1 serving: 294 Calories; 23.1 g Total Fat (8.9 g Mono, 1.5 g Poly, 11 g Sat); 90 mg Cholesterol; **2 g Carbohydrate**; trace Fibre; 19 g Protein; 197 mg Sodium

Note: Lamb chops may be broiled in oven. Place on greased broiler pan. Broil about 4 inches (10 cm) from heat in oven for 4 to 5 minutes per side until desired doneness.

1. Cucumber Salsa, page 79
2. Coconut Pork Stir-Fry, page 74
3. Cajun Pork Chops, page 79

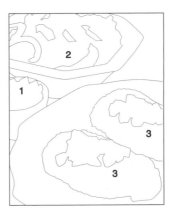

Crusted Pork Tenderloin

Tender, moist pork with an elegant walnut crust. An attractive dish for company.

Olive (or canola) oil	1 tsp.	5 mL
Pork tenderloin, trimmed of fat	1 lb.	454 g
Grated Parmesan cheese	1/2 cup	125 mL
Finely chopped walnuts, toasted (see Tip, page 24)	1/2 cup	125 mL
Hard margarine (or butter), softened	1 tbsp.	15 mL
Chopped fresh rosemary leaves (or 1/4 tsp., 1 mL, dried, crushed)	1 tsp.	5 mL
Salt	1/4 tsp.	1 mL
Pepper	1/4 tsp.	1 mL

Brush olive oil evenly over tenderloin.

Combine remaining 6 ingredients in large shallow baking dish. Press tenderloin into Parmesan cheese mixture until coated. Place on greased wire rack set in baking sheet with sides. Cover with foil. Cook in 375°F (190°C) oven for 10 minutes. Reduce heat to 350°F (175°C). Cook for 35 to 45 minutes until meat thermometer inserted into thickest part of tenderloin reads 155°F (68°C). Remove from oven. Cover with foil. Let stand for 10 minutes. Internal temperature should rise to at least 160°F (70°C). Serves 4.

1 serving: 338 Calories; 20.2 g Total Fat (7.3 g Mono, 7 g Poly, 4.9 g Sat); 77 mg Cholesterol; **3 g Carbohydrate**; 1 g Fibre; 37 g Protein; 485 mg Sodium

1. Grilled Chicken Salad, page 92
2. Tomato Tuna Salad, page 28
3. Shrimp And Sprouts, page 61

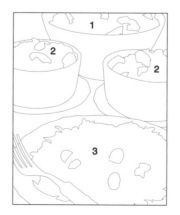

Coconut Pork Stir-Fry

Spicy hot coconut sauce seasons strips of pork tenderloin, red pepper and green beans. Colourful and very tasty.

Lime juice	1 tbsp.	15 mL
Cornstarch	1 1/2 tsp.	7 mL
Canola oil	1 tbsp.	15 mL
Pork tenderloin, trimmed of fat, cut into thin strips	1 lb.	454 g
Can of coconut milk	14 oz.	398 mL
Red curry paste	2 – 3 tsp.	10 – 15 mL
Fish sauce	1 tsp.	5 mL
Fresh (or frozen) whole green beans, cut into 2 inch (5 cm) pieces	1 cup	250 mL
Thinly sliced red pepper	1 cup	250 mL
Fresh spinach, stems removed, lightly packed	1 cup	250 mL
Chopped fresh basil (or 2 1/4 tsp., 11 mL, dried)	3 tbsp.	50 mL
Salted cashews, toasted (see Tip, page 24)	1/4 cup	60 mL

Stir lime juice into cornstarch in small cup until smooth. Set aside.

Heat wok or large frying pan on medium-high until very hot. Add canola oil. Add pork. Stir-fry for 3 to 4 minutes until desired doneness. Remove to medium bowl. Set aside.

Measure next 3 ingredients into same wok. Stir. Bring to a boil. Boil for 5 minutes, stirring occasionally.

Add green beans. Stir. Boil for 1 minute. Add red pepper. Cook for about 3 minutes, stirring occasionally, until vegetables are tender-crisp.

Add spinach and basil. Heat and stir for about 1 minute until spinach is wilted. Stir cornstarch mixture. Add to coconut milk mixture. Add pork. Stir-fry until heated through and sauce is thickened. Transfer to serving dish.

Sprinkle cashews over top. Serves 4.

1 serving: 454 Calories; 32.3 g Total Fat (7.4 g Mono, 2.7 g Poly, 20.1 g Sat); 67 mg Cholesterol; **13 g Carbohydrate**; 2 g Fibre; 32 g Protein; 229 mg Sodium

Pictured on page 71.

Black Bean Pork Ribs

Tender brown ribs in a rich, spicy sauce. Spoon the sauce over spaghetti squash for a delicious change!

Canola oil	1 tbsp.	15 mL
Sweet and sour cut pork ribs, trimmed of fat, cut into 1-bone portions (or pork button bones, see Note)	1 1/2 lbs.	680 g
Paprika	1 tsp.	5 mL
Salt	1/2 tsp.	2 mL
Pepper	1/8 tsp.	0.5 mL
Chili black bean sauce (see Note)	2 tbsp.	30 mL
Brown sugar, packed	1 tbsp.	15 mL
Low-sodium soy sauce	1 tbsp.	15 mL
Rice vinegar	1 tbsp.	15 mL
Garlic cloves, minced (or 1/2 tsp., 2 mL, powder)	2	2
Finely grated, peeled gingerroot	2 tsp.	10 mL
Water	1 1/2 cups	375 mL
Dry sherry	2 tbsp.	30 mL
Water	2 tbsp.	30 mL
Cornstarch	1 tbsp.	15 mL

Heat wok or large frying pan on medium-high until very hot. Add canola oil. Add next 4 ingredients. Stir-fry for about 5 minutes until ribs are browned. Remove ribs with slotted spoon to large plate.

Reduce heat to medium. Add next 6 ingredients. Heat and stir for 1 to 2 minutes until brown sugar is dissolved.

Add first amount of water and sherry. Stir. Bring to a boil. Add ribs. Reduce heat to medium-low. Cover. Simmer for 45 to 60 minutes until pork is tender.

Stir second amount of water into cornstarch in small cup until smooth. Add to pork mixture. Heat and stir for about 3 minutes until sauce is boiling and slightly thickened. Serves 4.

1 serving: 383 Calories; 26.9 g Total Fat (12.2 g Mono, 3.3 g Poly, 8.9 g Sat); 88 mg Cholesterol; **8 g Carbohydrate**; trace Fibre; 25 g Protein; 827 mg Sodium

Note: Button bones yield substantially more meat than same weight of ribs, but are sometimes difficult to find.

Note: Chili black bean sauce can be found in Asian section of most grocery stores.

Gypsy Stew

An old-world flavour combination—tender pork, sauerkraut and smoky bacon. Sour cream adds a mellowing touch to this unique stew.

Bacon slices, diced	6	6
Pork stew meat	1 1/2 lbs.	680 g
Large onions, halved lengthwise and thinly sliced	2	2
Paprika	4 tsp.	20 mL
Garlic cloves, minced (or 3/4 tsp., 4 mL, powder)	3	3
Caraway seed	1 tsp.	5 mL
Water	2 cups	500 mL
Salt	1/4 tsp.	1 mL
Sauerkraut, rinsed and drained well	2 cups	500 mL
Chicken bouillon powder	1 tsp.	5 mL
Light sour cream	1 cup	250 mL
All-purpose flour	2 tbsp.	30 mL

Cook bacon in large pot or Dutch oven on medium until almost crisp. Remove to paper towels to drain. Remove and discard drippings, reserving 1 tbsp. (15 mL) in pot. Return bacon to same pot.

Add next 5 ingredients. Heat and stir for about 10 minutes until onion is softened.

Add water and salt. Stir. Bring to a boil. Reduce heat to medium-low. Cover. Simmer for 1 hour, stirring occasionally.

Add sauerkraut and bouillon powder. Stir. Cover. Simmer for 45 to 60 minutes until pork is tender.

Combine sour cream and flour in small bowl until smooth. Slowly add to pork mixture, stirring constantly. Heat and stir for about 10 minutes until boiling and thickened. Serves 6.

1 serving: 394 Calories; 26.9 g Total Fat (12.3 g Mono, 3 g Poly, 11.8 g Sat); 94 mg Cholesterol; **13 g Carbohydrate**; 3 g Fibre; 25 g Protein; 748 mg Sodium

Ham And Cauliflower Bake

A versatile dish for any time of day. Creamy and cheesy!

Chopped cauliflower	4 1/2 cups	1.1 L
Boiling water		
Ice water		
Canola oil	2 tbsp.	30 mL
Diced cooked ham (about 1 1/2 lbs., 680 g)	4 cups	1 L
Diced red pepper	1 cup	250 mL
Can of condensed cream of asparagus soup	10 oz.	284 mL
Water	1/4 cup	60 mL
Chopped green onion	1/4 cup	60 mL
Pepper	1/2 tsp.	2 mL
Grated light sharp Cheddar cheese	1 cup	250 mL
Chopped fresh parsley (or 1/2 tsp., 2 mL, flakes)	2 tsp.	10 mL

Cook cauliflower in boiling water in large saucepan for about 5 minutes until tender-crisp. Drain. Immediately plunge into ice water in extra-large bowl. Let stand for about 10 minutes until cold. Drain. Set aside.

Heat canola oil in large frying pan on medium-high. Add ham and red pepper. Cook for about 5 minutes, stirring occasionally, until ham starts to brown.

Add next 4 ingredients. Heat and stir for 1 to 2 minutes until heated through. Transfer to greased 3 quart (3 L) shallow baking dish. Spread cauliflower evenly over top.

Sprinkle with cheese. Cook, uncovered, in 350°F (175°C) oven for about 35 minutes until heated through and cheese is melted.

Sprinkle with parsley. Serves 6.

1 serving: 366 Calories; 20.7 g Total Fat (9.3 g Mono, 3.9 g Poly, 6.8 g Sat); 81 mg Cholesterol; **11 g Carbohydrate**; 2 g Fibre; 33 g Protein; 2246 mg Sodium

Creamy Mushroom Pork

Thick, creamy mushroom sauce on pan-fried pork chops. Sauce has a subtle mustard finish everyone is sure to love.

Canola oil	1 tbsp.	15 mL
Boneless pork loin chops (about 1 lb., 454 g), trimmed of fat	4	4
Hard margarine (or butter)	1 tbsp.	15 mL
Sliced fresh white mushrooms	1 1/2 cups	375 mL
All-purpose flour	1 tbsp.	15 mL
Dry sherry	2 tbsp.	30 mL
Half-and-half cream (or homogenized milk)	1 cup	250 mL
Dijon mustard	1 tsp.	5 mL
Salt	1/4 tsp.	1 mL
Pepper	1/4 tsp.	1 mL

Heat canola oil in large frying pan on medium-high. Add pork chops. Cook for about 4 minutes per side until desired doneness. Remove to large serving dish. Cover to keep warm.

Reduce heat to medium. Melt margarine in same frying pan. Add mushrooms. Cook for about 5 minutes, stirring occasionally, until softened.

Add flour. Heat and stir for 1 minute. Add sherry. Stir until smooth.

Slowly add cream, stirring constantly. Add remaining 3 ingredients. Heat and stir for 2 to 3 minutes until boiling and thickened. Spoon over pork chops. Serves 4.

1 serving: 325 Calories; 20.3 g Total Fat (9.1 g Mono, 2.5 g Poly, 7.4 g Sat); 83 mg Cholesterol; **6 g Carbohydrate**; trace Fibre; 28 g Protein; 281 mg Sodium

Cajun Pork Chops

Cucumber salsa is the perfect side to cool the heat of these spicy chops.

Cajun seasoning	**2 tbsp.**	**30 mL**
All-purpose flour	**1 tbsp.**	**15 mL**
Pepper	**1/4 tsp.**	**1 mL**
Boneless pork loin chops (about 1 lb., 454 g), trimmed of fat	**4**	**4**
CUCUMBER SALSA		
English cucumber (with peel), cut in half lengthwise, seeds removed, chopped	**1/2 cup**	**125 mL**
Small tomato, quartered, seeds removed, chopped (about 1/3 cup, 75 mL)	**1**	**1**
Finely chopped red onion	**2 tbsp.**	**30 mL**
Plain yogurt	**2 tbsp.**	**30 mL**
Ground cumin	**1/8 tsp.**	**0.5 mL**
Salt	**1/8 tsp.**	**0.5 mL**

Combine first 3 ingredients in small cup. Rub on both sides of each pork chop. Preheat electric grill for 5 minutes or gas barbecue to medium (see Note). Cook pork chops on greased grill for 4 to 6 minutes per side until desired doneness. Transfer to large serving dish. Cover to keep warm.

Cucumber Salsa: Combine all 6 ingredients in small bowl. Makes about 3/4 cup (175 mL) salsa. Serve with pork chops. Serves 4.

1 serving: 205 Calories; 8.2 g Total Fat (3.4 g Mono, 0.9 g Poly, 2.6 g Sat); 63 mg Cholesterol; **6 g Carbohydrate**; 1 g Fibre; 26 g Protein; 763 mg Sodium

Pictured on page 71.

Note: Pork chops may be broiled in oven. Place on greased broiler pan. Broil about 4 inches (10 cm) from heat in oven for 4 to 6 minutes per side until desired doneness.

Greek Lamb Stir-Fry

A delicious way to prepare lamb. Marinating overnight will intensify the flavour of the meat.

ONION MARINADE		
Chopped onion	1/2 cup	125 mL
Dry white (or alcohol-free) wine	3 tbsp.	50 mL
Olive (or canola) oil	2 tbsp.	30 mL
Lemon juice	2 tsp.	10 mL
Dried whole oregano	1 tsp.	5 mL
Bay leaves, halved	2	2
Garlic powder	1/4 tsp.	1 mL
Salt	1/2 tsp.	2 mL
Pepper	1/2 tsp.	2 mL
Lamb stew meat	1 lb.	454 g
Fresh whole white mushrooms, larger ones cut in half	16	16
Canola oil	2 tsp.	10 mL

Onion Marinade: Combine first 9 ingredients in medium bowl. Makes about 1/2 cup (125 mL) marinade.

Put lamb and mushrooms into large resealable freezer bag. Pour marinade over top. Seal bag. Turn until coated. Marinate in refrigerator for 2 hours, turning occasionally. Drain and discard marinade. Remove and discard bay leaf halves.

Heat wok or large frying pan on medium-high until very hot. Add canola oil. Add lamb mixture. Stir-fry for 5 to 7 minutes until desired doneness. Serves 4.

1 serving: 234 Calories; 12.1 g Total Fat (6.3 g Mono, 1.7 g Poly, 2.8 g Sat); 74 mg Cholesterol; **6 g Carbohydrate**; 1 g Fibre; 25 g Protein; 226 mg Sodium

GREEK CHICKEN STIR-FRY: Omit lamb stew meat. Use same amount of chicken, cut into cubes. Stir-fry until chicken is no longer pink.

Orange-Glazed Lamb

Mildly spiced, glistening glaze coats these juicy lamb chops.

Rack of lamb, with 8 ribs	1 1/2 lbs.	680 g
Orange juice	3 tbsp.	50 mL
Orange marmalade	2 tbsp.	30 mL
Sweet chili sauce	2 tbsp.	30 mL
Dijon mustard (with whole seeds)	1 tbsp.	15 mL
Salt	1/4 tsp.	1 mL

(continued on next page)

Place lamb rack on greased wire rack set in foil-lined baking sheet with sides. Cover with foil. Cook in 350°F (175°C) oven for 35 to 45 minutes until desired doneness. Let stand for 10 minutes.

Combine remaining 5 ingredients in small saucepan. Heat and stir on medium-low for about 3 minutes until marmalade is melted. Let stand for 5 minutes. Cut lamb rack into individual chops. Place 2 chops on each of 4 individual plates. Spoon 1 tbsp. (15 mL) orange glaze over each lamb chop. Serves 4.

1 serving: 447 Calories; 29.8 g Total Fat (12.5 g Mono, 2.3 g Poly, 12.6 g Sat); 128 mg Cholesterol; **10 g Carbohydrate**; 1 g Fibre; 33 g Protein; 421 mg Sodium

Slow-Roasted Lamb

A warm, comforting dish to prepare when the days start to cool. The roasting time is long, but so worth the wait!

Whole leg of lamb roast, trimmed of fat	4 lbs.	1.8 kg
Garlic cloves, peeled and quartered	3	3
Olive (or canola) oil	1 tbsp.	15 mL
Dry red (or alcohol-free) wine	1/2 cup	125 mL
Low-sodium prepared chicken broth	1/2 cup	125 mL
Balsamic vinegar	1/4 cup	60 mL
Brown sugar, packed	2 tbsp.	30 mL
Salt	1/2 tsp.	2 mL

Cut 12 small slits in lamb roast. Insert 1 piece of garlic into each.

Heat olive oil in large frying pan on medium-high. Add lamb roast. Cook for about 8 minutes, turning often, until browned on all sides. Transfer to small roasting pan.

Measure remaining 5 ingredients into same frying pan. Heat and stir on medium, scraping any brown bits from bottom of pan, until brown sugar is dissolved. Pour wine mixture over lamb. Cover with foil. Cook in 250°F (120°C) oven for 4 to 4 1/2 hours, turning every hour, until lamb is tender. Transfer to serving dish. Cover with foil. Let stand for 15 minutes. Skim and discard fat from surface of liquid in roasting pan with spoon. Transfer liquid to small saucepan. Bring to a boil on medium. Reduce heat to medium-low. Simmer, uncovered, for 5 to 10 minutes until reduced by half. Makes about 1 1/4 cups (300 mL) sauce. Serve with lamb. Serves 6.

1 serving: 306 Calories; 11 g Total Fat (5.2 g Mono, 1 g Poly, 3.4 g Sat); 124 mg Cholesterol; **6 g Carbohydrate**; trace Fibre; 40 g Protein; 374 mg Sodium

Exotic Spiced Lamb Stew

Tender pieces of lamb in a rich tomato sauce. Exotic spices add a subtle curry flavour.

Canola oil	1 tbsp.	15 mL
Lamb stew meat	1 1/2 lbs.	680 g
Canola oil	1 tbsp.	15 mL
Chopped onion	1 cup	250 mL
Garlic cloves, minced (or 1/2 tsp., 2 mL, powder)	2	2
Ground cumin	2 tsp.	10 mL
Ground coriander	2 tsp.	10 mL
Ground ginger	1 tsp.	5 mL
Ground cardamom	1/2 tsp.	2 mL
Can of diced tomatoes (with juice)	14 oz.	398 mL
Low-sodium prepared beef broth	1 cup	250 mL
Brown sugar, packed	1/2 tsp.	2 mL
Sesame seeds, toasted (see Tip, page 24)	1 tbsp.	15 mL
Plain yogurt	1/2 cup	125 mL

Heat first amount of canola oil in large pot or Dutch oven on medium-high. Cook lamb in 2 to 3 batches for about 5 minutes per batch, stirring occasionally, until browned. Remove each batch to same large bowl. Set aside.

Reduce heat to medium. Heat second amount of canola oil in same pot. Add onion. Cook for 5 to 10 minutes, stirring often, until softened.

Add next 5 ingredients. Heat and stir for 1 to 2 minutes until fragrant.

Add lamb and next 3 ingredients. Bring to a boil. Reduce heat to low. Cover. Simmer for 1 1/2 hours, stirring occasionally. Increase heat to medium-low. Simmer, uncovered, for about 30 minutes, stirring occasionally, until lamb is tender and sauce is slightly thickened. Transfer to large serving dish.

Sprinkle with sesame seeds. Serve with yogurt. Serves 6.

1 serving: 250 Calories; 12.2 g Total Fat (5.6 g Mono, 2.4 g Poly, 2.8 g Sat); 75 mg Cholesterol; **9 g Carbohydrate**; 1 g Fibre; 26 g Protein; 314 mg Sodium

Hearty Beef Chili

Cream cheese adds a smooth touch to this filling chili. Brimming with tasty vegetables.

Bacon slices, diced	4	4
Cans of sliced mushrooms (10 oz., 284 mL, each), drained	2	2
Chopped celery	1 1/2 cups	375 mL
Chopped onion	1 cup	250 mL
Chopped zucchini (with peel)	1 cup	250 mL
Red medium pepper, chopped	1	1
Garlic cloves, minced (or 1/2 tsp., 2 mL, powder)	2	2
Lean ground beef	1 1/2 lbs.	680 g
Cans of red kidney beans (14 oz., 398 mL, each), drained and rinsed	2	2
Can of crushed tomatoes	14 oz.	398 mL
Low-sodium prepared beef broth	1 1/2 cups	375 mL
Chili powder	1 tbsp.	15 mL
Seasoned salt	2 tsp.	10 mL
Pepper	1/8 tsp.	0.5 mL
Block of light cream cheese, cut up	4 oz.	125 g
Grated light sharp Cheddar cheese (optional)	1/2 cup	125 mL

Cook bacon in large pot or Dutch oven on medium until crisp. Remove to paper towels to drain. Remove and discard drippings, reserving 1 tbsp. (15 mL) in pot.

Add next 6 ingredients. Cook for 5 to 10 minutes, stirring often, until onion is softened and vegetables are tender-crisp. Transfer to medium bowl.

Increase heat to medium-high. Add ground beef to same pot. Scramble-fry for 5 to 10 minutes until no longer pink. Drain.

Add mushroom mixture and next 6 ingredients. Stir. Bring to a boil. Reduce heat to medium-low. Cover. Simmer for 30 minutes, stirring occasionally.

Add bacon and cream cheese. Heat and stir for about 5 minutes until heated through and cream cheese is melted. Transfer to large serving bowl.

Sprinkle with Cheddar cheese. Serves 8.

1 serving: 315 Calories; 14.3 g Total Fat (5.7 g Mono, 1.1 g Poly, 5.9 g Sat); 57 mg Cholesterol; **23 g Carbohydrate**; 7 g Fibre; 25 g Protein; 1023 mg Sodium

Minted Lamb Salad

A sprinkling of mint and cumin is the perfect addition to this attractive salad.

GREEK MARINADE		
Lemon juice	2 tbsp.	30 mL
Olive (or canola) oil	2 tbsp.	30 mL
Garlic cloves, minced (or 1/2 tsp., 2 mL, powder)	2	2
Salt	1/4 tsp.	1 mL
Pepper	1/4 tsp.	1 mL
Lamb loin chops (about 12)	2 lbs.	900 g
Low-sodium prepared chicken broth	1/2 cup	125 mL
Couscous	1/2 cup	125 mL
Mixed salad greens, lightly packed	8 cups	2 L
Halved cherry tomatoes	1 1/2 cups	375 mL
Thinly sliced English cucumber (with peel)	1 cup	250 mL
Chopped fresh mint leaves (or 1 1/2 tsp., 7 mL, dried)	2 tbsp.	30 mL
YOGURT DRESSING		
Plain yogurt	2/3 cup	150 mL
Lemon juice	2 tbsp.	30 mL
Water	1 tbsp.	15 mL
Garlic clove, minced (or 1/4 tsp., 1 mL, powder)	1	1
Ground cumin	1/4 tsp.	1 mL
Salt, just a pinch		

Greek Marinade: Combine first 5 ingredients in small bowl. Makes about 1/4 cup (60 mL) marinade.

Put lamb chops into large resealable freezer bag. Pour marinade over top. Seal bag. Turn until coated. Marinate in refrigerator for at least 6 hours or overnight, turning occasionally. Drain and discard marinade. Preheat electric grill for 5 minutes or gas barbecue to medium (see Note). Cook lamb chops on greased grill for about 3 minutes per side until desired doneness. Remove from heat. Remove and discard bones. Thinly slice lamb. Transfer to extra-large bowl.

Heat broth in small saucepan on medium until hot. Add couscous. Stir. Cover. Remove from heat. Let stand for 5 minutes. Fluff with fork. Cool. Add to lamb.

Add next 4 ingredients. Toss.

Yogurt Dressing: Combine all 6 ingredients in small bowl. Makes about 1 cup (250 mL) dressing. Drizzle over salad greens mixture. Toss. Makes about 10 cups (2.5 L) salad. Serves 6.

(continued on next page)

1 serving: 381 Calories; 21.8 g Total Fat (9.7 g Mono, 1.8 g Poly, 8.6 g Sat); 82 mg Cholesterol; **20 g Carbohydrate**; 2 g Fibre; 26 g Protein; 209 mg Sodium

Pictured on page 107.

Note: Lamb chops may be broiled in oven. Place on greased broiler pan. Broil about 4 inches (10 cm) from heat in oven for about 3 minutes per side until desired doneness.

Turkey Chili

Chili made with turkey is a nice change of pace. Avocado salsa adds a tasty touch.

Canola oil	1 tbsp.	15 mL
Chopped onion	1 cup	250 mL
Chopped red pepper	1 cup	250 mL
Chopped celery	1/2 cup	125 mL
Garlic cloves, minced (or 1/2 tsp., 2 mL, powder)	2	2
Dried crushed chilies	2 tsp.	10 mL
Lean ground turkey	1 1/2 lbs.	680 g
Can of diced tomatoes (with juice)	28 oz.	796 mL
Can of red kidney beans, drained and rinsed	19 oz.	540 mL
Envelope of taco seasoning mix	1 1/4 oz.	35 g
AVOCADO SALSA		
Ripe large avocado, chopped	1	1
Medium tomato, chopped	1	1
Chopped green onion	1/4 cup	60 mL
Lemon juice	1 tbsp.	15 mL
Salt	1/4 tsp.	1 mL

Heat canola oil in large pot or Dutch oven on medium. Add next 5 ingredients. Cook for 5 to 10 minutes, stirring often, until onion is softened.

Add ground turkey. Scramble-fry for 8 to 10 minutes until turkey is no longer pink.

Add tomatoes, kidney beans and taco seasoning. Stir. Bring to a boil. Reduce heat to medium-low. Simmer, uncovered, for 35 to 45 minutes, stirring occasionally, until slightly thickened. Makes about 8 cups (2 L) chili.

Avocado Salsa: Combine all 5 ingredients in small bowl. Makes about 1 1/2 cups (375 mL) salsa. Serve with chili. Serves 8.

1 serving: 277 Calories; 13.5 g Total Fat (6.1 g Mono, 3 g Poly, 2.7 g Sat); 67 mg Cholesterol; **21 g Carbohydrate**; 5 g Fibre; 20 g Protein; 908 mg Sodium

Pictured on page 107.

Crustless Chicken Pie

Satisfying comfort food! A wonderfully saucy dish for any day of the week.

Canola oil	3 tbsp.	50 mL
Boneless, skinless chicken breast halves, cut into 1 inch (2.5 cm) pieces	1 lb.	454 g
Original no-salt seasoning (such as Mrs. Dash)	1 tsp.	5 mL
Chopped celery rib	1 cup	250 mL
Chopped onion	3/4 cup	175 mL
Garlic cloves, minced (or 1/2 tsp., 2 mL, powder)	2	2
Chopped peeled potato	1 cup	250 mL
Chopped green pepper	2/3 cup	150 mL
Chopped red pepper	2/3 cup	150 mL
Bay leaf	1	1
Dried savory	1/2 tsp.	2 mL
Low-sodium prepared chicken broth	1 cup	250 mL
All-purpose flour	3 tbsp.	50 mL
Light sour cream	1/4 cup	60 mL
Grated light medium Cheddar cheese	1/2 cup	125 mL
Grated Swiss cheese	1/2 cup	125 mL
Chopped fresh parsley, for garnish	2 tbsp.	30 mL

Heat canola oil in large frying pan on medium-high. Add chicken. Sprinkle with seasoning. Cook for about 5 minutes, stirring occasionally, until chicken is no longer pink. Remove chicken with slotted spoon to medium bowl. Set aside.

Reduce heat to medium. Add celery and onion to same frying pan. Cook for 5 to 10 minutes, stirring often, until softened.

Add garlic. Heat and stir for 1 to 2 minutes until fragrant.

Add chicken and next 5 ingredients. Stir.

Stir broth into flour in 2 cup (500 mL) liquid measure until smooth. Slowly add to chicken mixture, stirring constantly, until boiling and thickened. Reduce heat to medium-low. Cover. Simmer for about 25 minutes, stirring occasionally, until potato is tender. Remove and discard bay leaf.

Add sour cream. Stir. Transfer to greased 2 quart (2 L) casserole.

Sprinkle both cheeses over top. Bake, uncovered, in 425°F (220°C) oven for about 20 minutes until heated through and cheese is melted.

(continued on next page)

Sprinkle with parsley. Serves 4.

1 serving: 423 Calories; 20.6 g Total Fat (9.2 g Mono, 3.9 g Poly, 7.1 g Sat); 9˙ mg Cholesterol; **22 g Carbohydrate**; 3 g Fibre; 37 g Protein; 331 mg Sodium

Pictured on page 107.

Seafood Chowder

Tomato and fennel add fresh flavour to this hearty, chunky chowder.

Canola oil	2 tsp.	10 mL
Chopped fennel bulb (white part only)	1 cup	250 mL
Chopped onion	1/2 cup	125 mL
Chopped celery	1/2 cup	125 mL
Water	2 cups	500 mL
Can of diced tomatoes (with juice)	14 oz.	398 mL
Diced peeled potato	1 cup	250 mL
Diced green pepper	1 cup	250 mL
Granulated sugar	1 tsp.	5 mL
Bay leaves	2	2
Ground thyme	1/2 tsp.	2 mL
Salt	1/2 tsp.	2 mL
Pepper	1/2 tsp.	2 mL
Fresh (or frozen, thawed) cod fillets, cut into 1 inch (2.5 cm) pieces	1/2 lb.	225 g
Chopped cooked shrimp	1 cup	250 mL
Can of whole baby clams (with liquid)	5 oz.	142 g
Fresh (or frozen, thawed) small bay scallops	1/4 lb.	113 g

Heat canola oil in large saucepan on medium. Add next 3 ingredients. Cook for 5 to 10 minutes, stirring often, until vegetables are softened.

Add next 9 ingredients. Stir. Bring to a boil. Cook for about 10 minutes, stirring occasionally, until potato is tender.

Add cod. Reduce heat to medium-low. Cover. Simmer for 5 minutes.

Add remaining 3 ingredients. Stir. Simmer, uncovered, for about 2 minutes until fish flakes easily when tested with fork and scallops are opaque. Remove and discard bay leaves. Makes about 9 cups (2.25 L) chowder. Serves 6.

1 serving: 178 Calories; 4.3 g Total Fat (2 g Mono, 1.4 g Poly, 0.4 g Sat); 82 mg Cholesterol; **14 g Carbohydrate**; 2 g Fibre; 21 g Protein; 505 mg Sodium

Avocado Shrimp Salad

A colourful, summery salad coated with a sweet and tangy vinaigrette.

Cooked large shrimp	1 lb.	454 g
Ripe medium avocado, chopped	1	1
Thinly sliced English cucumber (with peel)	1 cup	250 mL
Thinly sliced red pepper	1 cup	250 mL
Thinly sliced celery	1 cup	250 mL
Sliced fresh peaches	1 cup	250 mL
Thinly sliced red onion	1/2 cup	125 mL
CHILI VINAIGRETTE		
Canola oil	3 tbsp.	50 mL
Red wine vinegar	2 tbsp.	30 mL
Chili sauce	2 tbsp.	30 mL
Chopped fresh chives (or 3/4 tsp., 4 mL, dried)	1 tbsp.	15 mL
Granulated sugar	2 tsp.	10 mL
Paprika	1/2 tsp.	2 mL
Salt	1/4 tsp.	1 mL

Put first 7 ingredients into extra-large bowl. Toss gently.

Chili Vinaigrette: Combine all 7 ingredients in jar with tight-fitting lid. Shake well. Makes about 1/2 cup (125 mL) vinaigrette. Drizzle over shrimp mixture. Toss gently. Makes about 8 cups (2 L) salad. Serves 4.

1 serving: 350 Calories; 19.6 g Total Fat (11.2 g Mono, 4.7 g Poly, 2.4 g Sat); 221 mg Cholesterol; **20 g Carbohydrate**; 4 g Fibre; 26 g Protein; 553 mg Sodium

Pictured on page 89.

1. Orange Pork And Rice, page 95
2. Italian Garden "Pasta," page 99
3. Avocado Shrimp Salad, above

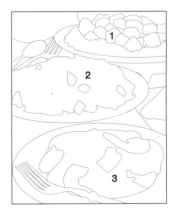

Thin-Crust Pizza

A crispy, golden-crusted pizza loaded with a rich assortment of toppings.

Phyllo pastry sheets	4	4
Hard margarine (or butter), melted	3 tbsp.	50 mL
Basil (or sun-dried tomato) pesto	2 tbsp.	30 mL
Fine dry bread crumbs	2 tbsp.	30 mL
Grated part-skim mozzarella cheese	1 cup	250 mL
Chopped cooked chicken	1 cup	250 mL
Diced cooked ham	1 cup	250 mL
Sliced roasted red peppers, drained and blotted dry	1/2 cup	125 mL
Thinly sliced red onion	1/2 cup	125 mL
Grated part-skim mozzarella cheese	1/2 cup	125 mL
Grated Parmesan cheese	2 tbsp.	30 mL

Work with pastry sheets 1 at a time. Keep remaining sheets covered with damp tea towel to prevent drying. Centre 1 pastry sheet on greased 12 inch (30 cm) pizza pan, letting pastry hang over edge. Brush with margarine. Repeat with remaining pastry sheets and margarine, arranging in spiral-fashion around pan. Scrunch or roll overhanging pastry inward to make an edge. Brush edge with margarine.

Spread pesto evenly over pastry base. Sprinkle bread crumbs over pesto.

Scatter remaining 7 ingredients, in order given, evenly over bread crumbs. Bake in 425°F (220°C) oven for 15 to 20 minutes until pastry is golden and cheese is melted. Let stand for 5 minutes. Cuts into 6 wedges.

1 wedge: 286 Calories; 16.4 g Total Fat (7.6 g Mono, 2 g Poly, 6 g Sat); 51 mg Cholesterol; **12 g Carbohydrate**; 1 g Fibre; 22 g Protein; 660 mg Sodium

Pictured on page 90.

1. Beef-Crusted Pizza, page 98
2. Thin-Crust Pizza, above

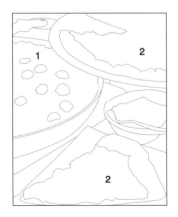

Grilled Chicken Salad

An inviting mixture of fresh vegetables glistens with a slightly sweet vinaigrette. Warm grilled chicken and crunchy walnuts make this salad irresistible!

Red medium peppers, quartered, seeds and ribs removed (see Note, page 93)	2	2
ZESTY BALSAMIC MARINADE		
Olive (or canola) oil	1 tbsp.	15 mL
Balsamic vinegar	1 tbsp.	15 mL
Finely grated orange zest	1 tsp.	5 mL
Salt	1/4 tsp.	1 mL
Pepper	1/4 tsp.	1 mL
Boneless, skinless chicken breast halves	3/4 lb.	340 g
Fresh spinach, stems removed, lightly packed	5 cups	1.25 L
Crumbled feta cheese (about 1/3 lb., 150 g)	1 cup	250 mL
Thinly sliced red onion	1/2 cup	125 mL
Coarsely chopped walnuts, toasted (see Tip, page 24)	1/4 cup	60 mL
BALSAMIC VINAIGRETTE		
Olive (or canola) oil	3 tbsp.	50 mL
Balsamic vinegar	1 tbsp.	15 mL
Chopped fresh oregano leaves (or 1/2 tsp., 2 mL, dried)	2 tsp.	10 mL
Garlic clove, minced (or 1/4 tsp., 1 mL, powder)	1	1
Salt, just a pinch		

Preheat electric grill for 5 minutes or gas barbecue to medium-high. Cook peppers, skin-side down, on greased grill for 10 to 12 minutes until skins are blistered and blackened. Transfer to small bowl. Cover with plastic wrap. Let sweat for about 15 minutes until cool enough to handle. Peel and discard skins. Cut into thin strips. Set aside.

Zesty Balsamic Marinade: Combine first 5 ingredients in small cup. Makes about 2 tbsp. (30 mL) marinade.

Place chicken breast halves in medium resealable freezer bag. Pour marinade over top. Seal bag. Turn until coated. Marinate in refrigerator for 1 to 3 hours, turning occasionally. Drain and discard marinade. Heat electric grill for 5 minutes or gas barbecue to medium. Cook chicken on greased grill for about 5 minutes per side until no longer pink inside. Cool. Cut into thin slices. Transfer to large bowl.

Add red pepper and next 4 ingredients. Toss.

(continued on next page)

Balsamic Vinaigrette: Combine all 5 ingredients in jar with tight-fitting lid. Shake well. Makes about 1/4 cup (60 mL) vinaigrette. Drizzle over spinach mixture. Toss. Makes about 8 cups (2 L) salad. Serves 4.

1 serving: 425 Calories; 27.2 g Total Fat (12.1 g Mono, 5 g Poly, 8.3 g Sat); 96 mg Cholesterol; **13 g Carbohydrate**; 4 g Fibre; 34 g Protein; 571 mg Sodium

Pictured on page 72.

Note: Prepared roasted red peppers are available in jars in most grocery stores. Drain well. Use 1 cup (250 mL) in place of 2 fresh, roasted red peppers.

Oriental Chicken Salad

Make the dressing and cook the chicken the day before for quick and easy assembly when company arrives.

ORIENTAL DRESSING

Reserved juice from mandarin orange segments	2/3 cup	150 mL
Rice vinegar	1/2 cup	125 mL
Low-sodium soy sauce	1/4 cup	60 mL
Low-calorie sweetener (Splenda)	3 tbsp.	50 mL
Finely grated, peeled gingerroot	1 tbsp.	15 mL
Chili paste (sambal oelek)	2 – 3 tsp.	10 – 15 mL
Boneless, skinless chicken breast halves	1 lb.	454 g
Shredded suey choy (Chinese cabbage), lightly packed	8 cups	2 L
Can of mandarin orange segments, drained and juice reserved	10 oz.	284 mL
Sliced red pepper	1 cup	250 mL
Dry chow mein noodles	1/2 cup	125 mL

Oriental Dressing: Combine first 6 ingredients in medium bowl. Makes 1 1/2 cups (375 mL) dressing. Reserve 2 tbsp. (30 mL) dressing in small cup. Chill remaining dressing.

Arrange chicken breast halves in greased 9 x 9 inch (22 x 22 cm) pan. Brush with reserved dressing. Cook, uncovered, in 375°F (190°C) oven for 20 to 25 minutes until chicken is no longer pink inside. Cool. Cut into thin slices. Transfer to large bowl.

Add next 3 ingredients. Toss. Drizzle chilled dressing over cabbage mixture. Toss.

Sprinkle with chow mein noodles. Makes about 12 cups (3 L) salad. Serves 6.

1 serving: 177 Calories; 3.1 g Total Fat (0.7 g Mono, 1.2 g Poly, 0.7 g Sat); 54 mg Cholesterol; **15 g Carbohydrate**; 2 g Fibre; 24 g Protein; 374 mg Sodium

Chicken Lentil Cacciatore

Hearty tomato sauce adds zip to tender chicken and lentils. A well-balanced combination in one dish for dinner!

Olive (or canola) oil	1 tbsp.	15 mL
Boneless, skinless chicken thighs (about 1 1/2 lbs., 680 g)	8	8
Olive (or canola) oil	1 tbsp.	15 mL
Sliced fresh white mushrooms	1 1/2 cups	375 mL
Chopped onion	1 cup	250 mL
Chopped red pepper	3/4 cup	175 mL
Garlic cloves, minced (or 1/2 tsp., 2 mL, powder)	2	2
Can of diced tomatoes (with juice)	28 oz.	796 mL
Low-sodium prepared chicken broth	1 cup	250 mL
Red lentils	1/2 cup	125 mL
Tomato paste (see Tip, page 44)	2 tbsp.	30 mL
Salt	1/4 tsp.	1 mL
Pepper	1/4 tsp.	1 mL
Chopped zucchini (with peel)	1 cup	250 mL
Pitted kalamata olives (Greek), optional	1/4 cup	60 mL
Chopped fresh parsley (or 2 1/4 tsp., 11 mL, flakes)	3 tbsp.	50 mL

Heat first amount of olive oil in large pot or Dutch oven on medium-high. Add chicken thighs. Cook for 8 to 10 minutes, turning occasionally, until browned on all sides. Remove to large plate.

Reduce heat to medium. Heat second amount of olive oil in same pot. Add next 4 ingredients. Cook for 5 to 10 minutes, stirring often, until onion is softened.

Add next 6 ingredients. Stir. Return chicken to pot. Bring to a boil. Reduce heat to medium-low. Cover. Simmer for about 30 minutes until chicken is no longer pink inside and lentils are softened.

Add remaining 3 ingredients. Stir. Cover. Simmer for about 5 minutes until zucchini is tender-crisp. Serves 6.

1 serving: 257 Calories; 9.4 g Total Fat (4.7 g Mono, 1.7 g Poly, 1.8 g Sat); 63 mg Cholesterol; **22 g Carbohydrate**; 4 g Fibre; 22 g Protein; 434 mg Sodium

Orange Pork And Rice

When you want something just a bit different, try this dish. Fantastic flavour!

Orange juice	3/4 cup	175 mL
Cornstarch	1 tbsp.	15 mL
Low-sodium soy sauce	3 tbsp.	50 mL
Brown sugar, packed	1 tbsp.	15 mL
Garlic clove, minced (or 1/4 tsp., 1 mL, powder)	1	1
Finely grated, peeled gingerroot (or 1/4 tsp., 1 mL, ground ginger)	1 tsp.	5 mL
Canola oil	2 tbsp.	30 mL
Lean boneless pork loin, cut into 1 inch (2.5 cm) cubes	1 1/2 lbs.	680 g
Canola oil	2 tbsp.	30 mL
Can of sliced mushrooms, drained	10 oz.	284 mL
Sliced green pepper	1 cup	250 mL
Chopped onion	1/4 cup	60 mL
Cooked wild rice (about 3/4 cup, 175 mL, uncooked)	2 cups	500 mL
Chopped fresh basil (or 3/4 tsp., 4 mL, dried)	1 tbsp.	15 mL

Stir orange juice into cornstarch in small bowl until smooth. Add next 4 ingredients. Stir. Set aside.

Heat first amount of canola oil in large frying pan on medium-high. Add pork. Cook for 5 to 10 minutes, turning occasionally, until browned on all sides. Stir orange juice mixture. Add to pork. Heat and stir until boiling and slightly thickened. Transfer to large serving bowl. Cover to keep warm.

Heat second amount of canola oil in same frying pan on medium-high. Add next 3 ingredients. Cook for about 5 minutes, stirring often, until green pepper is tender-crisp.

Add rice and basil. Heat and stir for about 2 minutes until heated through. Transfer to large serving dish. Top with pork mixture. Serves 6.

1 serving: 330 Calories; 12.5 g Total Fat (6.8 g Mono, 3.2 g Poly, 1.7 g Sat); 67 mg Cholesterol; **24 g Carbohydrate**; 1 g Fibre; 31 g Protein; 405 mg Sodium

Pictured on page 89.

Mushroom Squash Frittata

Bold blue cheese complements sweet squash. Wonderful for lunch with a mixed green salad.

Butternut squash, cut into 1/2 inch (12 mm) cubes	2 lbs.	900 g
Water		
Salt	1/2 tsp.	2 mL
Olive (or canola) oil	1 tbsp.	15 mL
Hard margarine (or butter)	2 tsp.	10 mL
Sliced fresh white mushrooms	2 cups	500 mL
Sliced green onion	1/2 cup	125 mL
Garlic cloves, minced (or 1/2 tsp., 2 mL, powder)	2	2
Large eggs	8	8
Milk (or half-and-half cream)	1/2 cup	125 mL
Salt	1/4 tsp.	1 mL
Pepper	1/4 tsp.	1 mL
Crumbled blue cheese (about 2 oz., 58 g)	1/2 cup	125 mL
Walnut pieces, toasted (see Tip, page 24)	1/3 cup	75 mL

Cook squash in water and first amount of salt in large saucepan until just tender. Drain. Set aside.

Heat olive oil and margarine in large frying pan on medium. Add mushrooms. Cook for about 5 minutes, stirring often, until mushrooms are softened and liquid is evaporated.

Add onion and garlic. Heat and stir for 1 to 2 minutes until fragrant. Add squash. Stir well. Spread evenly in greased 3 quart (3 L) casserole.

Beat next 4 ingredients with whisk in large bowl. Pour over squash mixture.

Scatter cheese and walnuts over top. Cook in 350°F (175°C) oven for about 30 minutes until set. Serves 6.

1 serving: 289 Calories; 17.9 g Total Fat (6.9 g Mono, 4.2 g Poly, 5.1 g Sat); 296 mg Cholesterol; **20 g Carbohydrate**; 3 g Fibre; 15 g Protein; 363 mg Sodium

Peppered Beef Pot Roast

Tender pot roast accompanied by peppery sauce and vegetables.

Olive (or canola) oil	1 tbsp.	15 mL
Boneless beef cross rib roast	3 lbs.	1.4 kg
Olive (or canola) oil	1 tbsp.	15 mL
Thinly sliced onion	2 cups	500 mL
Chopped carrot	2 cups	500 mL
Chopped parsnip	2 cups	500 mL
Low-sodium prepared beef broth	1 cup	250 mL
Dry red (or alcohol-free) wine	1/2 cup	125 mL
Whole black peppercorns, cracked (see Tip, below)	2 tsp.	10 mL
Salt	1/2 tsp.	2 mL
Fresh (or frozen) whole green beans, cut into 1 inch (2.5 cm) pieces	2 cups	500 mL
Chopped fresh parsley (or 2 1/4 tsp., 11 mL, flakes)	3 tbsp.	50 mL

Heat first amount of olive oil in large pot or Dutch oven on medium-high. Add roast. Cook for 5 to 8 minutes, turning occasionally, until browned on all sides. Remove to large plate.

Reduce heat to medium. Heat second amount of olive oil in same pot. Add onion. Cook for 5 to 10 minutes, stirring often, until softened.

Add next 6 ingredients. Stir. Return roast to pot. Bring to a boil. Reduce heat to medium-low. Cover. Simmer for about 2 hours, turning roast halfway through cooking time, until desired doneness. Remove roast to large serving plate. Cover with foil. Let stand for 15 minutes. Increase heat to medium-high. Bring liquid remaining in pot to a boil. Boil, uncovered, for 10 to 15 minutes, stirring occasionally, until slightly thickened.

Add green beans and parsley. Stir. Cover. Cook for 3 to 5 minutes until beans are tender-crisp. Serve with beef. Serves 8 to 10.

1 serving: 500 Calories; 31.1 g Total Fat (14.3 g Mono, 1.5 g Poly, 11.7 g Sat); 94 mg Cholesterol; **17 g Carbohydrate**; 4 g Fibre; 35 g Protein; 360 mg Sodium

To crack peppercorns, place whole peppercorns in small plastic bag. Tap peppercorns with heavy object, such as meat mallet or hammer, until cracked.

Beef-Crusted Pizza

A spicy, meat-lover's pizza with lots of cheese! Add your favourite toppings for variety.

Lean ground beef	1 1/2 lbs.	680 g
Grated part-skim mozzarella cheese	1/3 cup	75 mL
Fine dry bread crumbs	1/4 cup	60 mL
Large eggs, fork-beaten	2	2
Dried basil	2 tsp.	10 mL
Dried whole oregano	1 tsp.	5 mL
Pepper	1 tsp.	5 mL
Dried thyme	1/2 tsp.	2 mL
Tomato sauce	1/3 cup	75 mL
Grated part-skim mozzarella cheese	2/3 cup	150 mL
Medium tomato, sliced	1	1
Can of sliced ripe olives, drained	4 1/2 oz.	125 mL
Chopped green pepper	1/2 cup	125 mL
Grated Monterey Jack With Jalapeño cheese	2/3 cup	150 mL

Scramble-fry ground beef in large non-stick frying pan on medium-high for 5 to 10 minutes until no longer pink. Drain. Transfer beef to large bowl. Cool.

Add next 7 ingredients. Stir well. Press beef mixture in bottom and halfway up side of greased 12 inch (30 cm) deep dish pizza pan. Bake in 400°F (205°C) oven for about 5 minutes until firm and cheese is melted. Let stand for 10 minutes.

Spoon tomato sauce onto beef crust. Spread evenly. Sprinkle second amount of mozzarella cheese over sauce. Layer next 3 ingredients, in order given, over cheese.

Sprinkle with Monterey Jack cheese. Bake for 15 to 20 minutes until cheese is melted and golden. Cuts into 6 wedges.

1 wedge: 341 Calories; 19.6 g Total Fat (7.5 g Mono, 1 g Poly, 9 g Sat); 154 mg Cholesterol; **8 g Carbohydrate**; 1 g Fibre; 32 g Protein; 426 mg Sodium

Pictured on page 90.

Italian Garden "Pasta"

A tempting tomato and herb sauce coats spicy sausage and zucchini "noodles" in this savoury dish.

Canola oil	2 tsp.	10 mL
Hot Italian sausage, cut into 1/4 inch (6 mm) thick slices	1/2 lb.	225 g
Chopped onion	1/4 cup	60 mL
Garlic cloves, minced (or 1/2 tsp., 2 mL, powder)	2	2
Can of diced tomatoes (with juice)	14 oz.	398 mL
Diced red pepper	1/2 cup	125 mL
Dried whole oregano	1 tsp.	5 mL
Dried basil	1 tsp.	5 mL
Dried thyme	1/2 tsp.	2 mL
Canola oil	1 tbsp.	15 mL
Small zucchini, peeled into 4 inch (10 cm) long ribbons with vegetable peeler	4	4
Grated Parmesan cheese	1/3 cup	75 mL

Heat first amount of canola oil in large saucepan on medium. Add sausage. Cook for about 4 minutes, stirring occasionally, until sausage starts to brown.

Add onion and garlic. Heat and stir for about 2 minutes until fragrant.

Add next 5 ingredients. Stir. Bring to a boil. Reduce heat to medium-low. Simmer, uncovered, for about 15 minutes until red pepper and onion are softened.

Heat second amount of canola oil in large non-stick frying pan on medium-high. Add zucchini. Heat and stir for about 3 minutes until softened. Remove from heat. Cover. Let stand for 10 minutes. Drain and discard liquid. Add zucchini to sausage mixture. Toss. Transfer to large serving bowl.

Sprinkle with Parmesan cheese. Serves 4.

1 serving: 340 Calories; 26.6 g Total Fat (12.3 g Mono, 4.3 g Poly, 8.5 g Sat); 50 mg Cholesterol; **12 g Carbohydrate**; 4 g Fibre; 15 g Protein; 745 mg Sodium

Pictured on page 89.

Zucchini And Chicken Dish

Chunks of chicken and ribbons of zucchini smothered in cheese make a satisfying meal everyone will love. Zucchini may be diced, if preferred.

Olive (or canola) oil	2 tbsp.	30 mL
Boneless, skinless chicken breast halves, diced	1 lb.	454 g
Lemon pepper	1/4 tsp.	1 mL
Garlic cloves, minced (or 1/2 tsp., 2 mL, powder)	2	2
All-purpose flour	1 tbsp.	15 mL
Can of stewed tomatoes (with juice), puréed	14 oz.	398 mL
Dried basil	1/2 tsp.	2 mL
Dried whole oregano	1/4 tsp.	1 mL
Low-sodium prepared chicken broth	2 cups	500 mL
Small zucchini, peeled into 4 inch (10 cm) long ribbons with vegetable peeler	4	4
Frozen French-style green beans, thawed	2 cups	500 mL
Grated part-skim mozzarella cheese	1 cup	250 mL
Grated Parmesan (or Romano) cheese	1/4 cup	60 mL

Heat olive oil in large frying pan on medium-high. Add chicken. Sprinkle with lemon pepper. Cook for about 5 minutes, stirring often, until chicken is no longer pink.

Reduce heat to medium. Add garlic. Heat and stir for 1 to 2 minutes until fragrant.

Add flour. Heat and stir for 1 minute.

Add puréed tomato, basil and oregano. Stir until boiling and slightly thickened. Reduce heat to medium-low. Simmer, uncovered, for 10 minutes, stirring occasionally. Remove from heat. Cover to keep warm.

Measure broth into large saucepan. Bring to a boil on medium. Add zucchini. Stir. Cover. Cook for about 4 minutes until tender. Remove zucchini with slotted spoon to greased 3 quart (3 L) shallow baking dish, reserving broth in saucepan.

Return broth to a boil. Add green beans. Stir. Cover. Cook for about 5 minutes until tender. Remove beans with slotted spoon to same baking dish (see Note). Spread evenly over zucchini. Spoon chicken mixture evenly over vegetables.

Sprinkle with both cheeses. Cook, uncovered, in 350°F (175°C) oven for about 30 minutes until cheese is melted and bubbling. Serves 4.

(continued on next page)

1 serving: 383 Calories; 16.3 g Total Fat (7.5 g Mono, 1.4 g Poly, 5.9 g Sat); 89 mg Cholesterol; **20 g Carbohydrate**; 4 g Fibre; 41 g Protein; 866 mg Sodium

Note: After cooking vegetables, use remaining chicken broth to make Crustless Chicken Pie, page 86, or Chicken Lentil Cacciatore, page 94.

Roasted Veggies And Lentils

Enjoy this meatless low-carb dish, full of flavour and colour.

Medium zucchini (with peel), cut crosswise into 1 inch (2.5 cm) slices	2	2
Red medium pepper, seeds and ribs removed, cut into 1 inch (2.5 cm) pieces	1	1
Yellow medium pepper, seeds and ribs removed, cut into 1 inch (2.5 cm) pieces	1	1
Small red onion, cut into 1 inch (2.5 cm) pieces	1	1
Garlic cloves (with peel), bruised (see Tip, page 105), or 1 tsp. (5 mL) powder	4	4
Sprigs of fresh rosemary	2	2
Olive (or canola) oil	2 tbsp.	30 mL
Salt	1/2 tsp.	2 mL
Pepper	1/2 tsp.	2 mL
Can of lentils, drained and rinsed	19 oz.	540 mL
Grated light sharp Cheddar cheese	1 cup	250 mL

Combine first 9 ingredients in large bowl. Spread evenly in greased baking sheet with sides. Cook in 425°F (220°C) oven for 20 to 25 minutes, turning occasionally, until vegetables are tender. Remove and discard garlic cloves and rosemary sprigs.

Scatter lentils evenly over vegetables. Sprinkle with cheese. Broil about 4 inches (10 cm) from heat in oven for 3 to 5 minutes until heated through and cheese is melted and golden. Serves 4.

1 serving: 274 Calories; 13.4 g Total Fat (6.9 g Mono, 0.9 g Poly, 4.8 g Sat); 18 mg Cholesterol; **24 g Carbohydrate**; 6 g Fibre; 16 g Protein; 662 mg Sodium

Chorizo Chicken

Colourful and aromatic with a nice, mild heat.

Olive (or canola) oil	1 tbsp.	15 mL
Bone-in, skinless chicken thighs (3 – 4 oz., 85 – 113 g, each)	8	8
Diced chorizo sausage (about 1)	3/4 cup	175 mL
Olive (or canola) oil	2 tsp.	10 mL
Chopped red onion	1 cup	250 mL
Chopped red pepper	1 cup	250 mL
Garlic cloves, minced	4	4
Chopped tomato	1 cup	250 mL
Low-sodium prepared chicken broth	3/4 cup	175 mL
Long grain brown rice	1/3 cup	75 mL
Pepper	1/4 tsp.	1 mL
Frozen peas	1/2 cup	125 mL
Chopped fresh basil (or 1 1/2 tsp., 7 mL, dried)	2 tbsp.	30 mL
Grated Parmesan cheese	1/4 cup	60 mL
Pine nuts, toasted (see Tip, page 24), optional	1 tbsp.	15 mL

Heat first amount of olive oil in large frying pan on medium. Add chicken thighs. Cook for 8 to 10 minutes, turning occasionally, until browned on all sides. Remove to large plate. Set aside.

Add chorizo to same frying pan. Cook for 3 to 5 minutes, stirring occasionally, until lightly browned. Remove to paper towels to drain. Remove and discard any drippings from pan.

Heat second amount of olive oil in same frying pan on medium. Add onion and red pepper. Cook for 5 to 10 minutes, stirring often, until onion is softened.

Add garlic. Heat and stir for 1 to 2 minutes until fragrant.

Add next 4 ingredients. Stir. Bring to a boil. Add chicken and chorizo. Reduce heat to medium-low. Cover. Simmer for 40 to 45 minutes until rice is tender and chicken is no longer pink inside.

Add peas and basil. Stir. Cover. Cook for about 5 minutes until peas are tender. Transfer to large serving dish.

Sprinkle Parmesan cheese and pine nuts over top. Serves 4.

1 serving: 347 Calories; 15.4 g Total Fat (7.4 g Mono, 2.3 g Poly, 4.1 g Sat); 93 mg Cholesterol; **25 g Carbohydrate**; 3 g Fibre; 27 g Protein; 315 mg Sodium

Corned Beef And Sauerkraut

This will remind you of a Reuben sandwich—without the bread!

Medium potatoes, peeled and quartered	3	3
Water		
Milk	1/4 cup	60 mL
Hard margarine (or butter)	1/2 tbsp.	7 mL
Salt	1/16 tsp.	0.5 mL
Pepper, sprinkle		
Hard margarine (or butter)	1 tbsp.	15 mL
Medium onion, thinly sliced	1	1
Jar of sauerkraut, rinsed and drained well	17 1/2 oz.	500 mL
Deli corned beef, cut into thin strips (about 3 cups, 750 mL)	13 1/2 oz.	384 g
Paprika	1/4 tsp.	1 mL
Caraway seed	1/4 tsp.	1 mL
Grated Swiss cheese	1 cup	250 mL

Cook potatoes in water in large saucepan until tender. Drain. Mash.

Add next 4 ingredients. Mix well. Set aside.

Melt second amount of margarine in large frying pan on medium. Add onion. Cook for 5 to 10 minutes, stirring often, until softened.

Add sauerkraut. Heat and stir for about 3 minutes until liquid is evaporated. Add to potato mixture. Stir. Spread evenly in greased 2 quart (2 L) casserole.

Put next 3 ingredients into medium bowl. Stir. Scatter evenly over sauerkraut mixture.

Sprinkle with cheese. Cook, uncovered, in 350°F (175°C) oven for 35 to 45 minutes until heated through and cheese is melted. Serves 6.

1 serving: 295 Calories; 15.2 g Total Fat (6.6 g Mono, 0.8 g Poly, 6.4 g Sat); 81 mg Cholesterol; **20 g Carbohydrate**; 3 g Fibre; 20 g Protein; 1172 mg Sodium

Cucumber Sesame Salad

An elegant, crisp salad with an Asian flair. Colourful and light!

English cucumber (with peel), cut in half lengthwise	1	1
Thinly sliced radish	1 cup	250 mL
Sesame seeds, toasted (see Tip, page 24)	2 tbsp.	30 mL
SESAME DRESSING		
Canola oil	1 1/2 tbsp.	25 mL
White wine vinegar	1 tbsp.	15 mL
Sweet chili sauce	1 tbsp.	15 mL
Granulated sugar	1 tsp.	5 mL
Fish sauce	1/4 tsp.	1 mL
Sesame oil, for flavour	1/4 tsp.	1 mL

Remove and discard seeds from cucumber with spoon. Slice each half diagonally into 1/4 inch (6 mm) thick slices. Transfer to medium bowl.

Add radish and sesame seeds. Toss.

Sesame Dressing: Combine all 6 ingredients in jar with tight-fitting lid. Shake well. Makes 1/4 cup (60 mL) dressing. Drizzle over cucumber mixture. Toss. Makes about 3 1/2 cups (875 mL) salad. Serves 4.

1 serving: 101 Calories; 8 g Total Fat (4 g Mono, 2.7 g Poly, 0.8 g Sat); 0 mg Cholesterol; **7 g Carbohydrate**; 2 g Fibre; 2 g Protein; 91 mg Sodium

Roasted Turnip

Tender, mildly spiced turnip complemented by mellow roasted garlic. A tasty addition to a roast beef dinner!

Garlic cloves, bruised (see Tip, below)	8	8
Olive (or canola) oil	2 tbsp.	30 mL
Fennel seed	2 tsp.	10 mL
Salt	1/2 tsp.	2 mL
Coarse ground pepper	1/2 tsp.	2 mL
Yellow turnip, cut into 1/2 inch (12 mm) cubes (about 4 1/4 cups, 1.1 L)	2 lbs.	900 g

Combine first 5 ingredients in large bowl.

Add turnip. Toss until coated. Spread evenly in greased baking sheet with sides. Cook in 375°F (190°C) oven for 35 to 40 minutes, stirring occasionally, until turnip is tender. Remove garlic cloves to small plate. Carefully remove and discard peel. Mash garlic with fork. Transfer turnip mixture to large serving bowl. Add garlic. Toss gently. Serves 4.

1 serving: 123 Calories; 7.2 g Total Fat (5.2 g Mono, 0.7 g Poly, 1 g Sat); 0 mg Cholesterol; **14 g Carbohydrate**; 3 g Fibre; 2 g Protein; 421 mg Sodium

Pictured on page 108.

To bruise garlic, hit cloves with mallet or press with flat side of wide knife to "bruise" or crack them open slightly.

Cheesy Spiced Tomatoes

These will add a bit of zing to any meal! Great with grilled beef or chicken. Use firm tomatoes for best results.

Medium tomatoes, halved crosswise	2	2
Balsamic vinegar	1 tsp.	5 mL
Hot pepper sauce	1/2 tsp.	2 mL
Finely chopped fresh basil (or 1/2 tsp., 2 mL, dried)	2 tsp.	10 mL
Salt, sprinkle		
Pepper, sprinkle		
Grated Parmesan cheese	6 tbsp.	100 mL

Place tomato halves, cut-side up, on greased broiler pan or baking sheet with sides. Drizzle balsamic vinegar and hot pepper sauce over top of each.

Divide and sprinkle remaining 4 ingredients, in order given, on each tomato half. Broil about 6 inches (15 cm) from heat in oven for 5 to 10 minutes until cheese is bubbling and golden. Serves 4.

1 serving: 57 Calories; 3.1 g Total Fat (0.9 g Mono, 0.2 g Poly, 1.8 g Sat); 7 mg Cholesterol; **3 g Carbohydrate**; 1 g Fibre; 4 g Protein; 198 mg Sodium

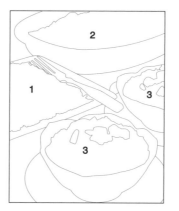

Bacon Brussels Sprouts

A delightful way to dress up Brussels sprouts.

Brussels sprouts (about 1 1/2 lbs., 680 g)	**5 cups**	**1.25 L**
Water		
Hard margarine (or butter)	**2 tbsp.**	**30 mL**
Bacon slices, cooked crisp and crumbled	**4**	**4**
Slivered almonds, toasted (see Tip, page 24)	**3 tbsp.**	**50 mL**
Dijon mustard	**1 tsp.**	**5 mL**

Cook Brussels sprouts in water in large saucepan on medium until tender-crisp. Drain. Transfer to large bowl. Cover to keep warm.

Melt margarine in same large saucepan on medium. Add remaining 3 ingredients. Stir. Add to Brussels sprouts. Toss gently. Serves 6.

1 serving: 117 Calories; 8.4 g Total Fat (4.9 g Mono, 1.2 g Poly, 1.8 g Sat); 4 mg Cholesterol; **8 g Carbohydrate**; 3 g Fibre; 5 g Protein; 146 mg Sodium

Pictured on page 108.

1. Lemon Dill Tomatoes, page 118
2. Bacon Brussels Sprouts, above
3. Roasted Turnip, page 105

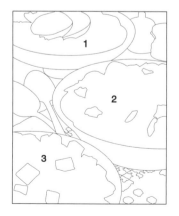

Mushrooms In Cream Sauce

Wonderful flavour, with a hint of sherry. Great on steak, or served with pork chops.

Canola oil	1 tbsp.	15 mL
Sliced fresh brown (or white) mushrooms	4 cups	1 L
Salt	1/4 tsp.	1 mL
Pepper	1/4 tsp.	1 mL
Garlic cloves, minced (or 1/2 tsp., 2 mL, powder)	2	2
Dry sherry	2 tbsp.	30 mL
Whipping cream	3/4 cup	175 mL
Chopped fresh parsley (or 1 1/2 tsp., 7 mL, flakes)	2 tbsp.	30 mL

Heat canola oil in large frying pan on medium-high. Add mushrooms, salt and pepper. Cook for about 5 minutes, stirring occasionally, until mushrooms are softened and just starting to brown.

Add garlic. Heat and stir for 1 to 2 minutes until fragrant.

Add sherry. Heat and stir for about 1 minute until sherry is almost evaporated. Slowly add whipping cream, stirring constantly, until boiling and thickened.

Add parsley. Stir. Serves 4.

1 serving: 201 Calories; 19 g Total Fat (6.5 g Mono, 1.6 g Poly, 9.8 g Sat); 55 mg Cholesterol; **6 g Carbohydrate**; 1 g Fibre; 3 g Protein; 170 mg Sodium

Grilled Balsamic Asparagus

Tender-crisp asparagus grilled to perfection with a zesty balsamic vinegar sauce.

Fresh asparagus, trimmed of tough ends	1 lb.	454 g
Water		
Ice water		
Balsamic vinegar	1 1/2 tbsp.	25 mL
Low-calorie sweetener (Splenda), optional	1 1/2 tsp.	7 mL
Olive (or canola) oil	1 tbsp.	15 mL
Salt	1/2 tsp.	2 mL

(continued on next page)

Cook asparagus in boiling water in large frying pan on medium until just tender-crisp. Drain. Immediately plunge into ice water in large bowl. Let stand for about 5 minutes until cool. Drain. Blot with paper towels. Transfer to large plate.

Combine remaining 4 ingredients in small cup. Brush balsamic vinegar mixture evenly over asparagus. Preheat electric grill for 5 minutes or gas barbecue to medium. Place asparagus crosswise on greased grill. Cook for 3 to 4 minutes, turning occasionally and brushing with remaining balsamic vinegar mixture, until tender-crisp. Serves 4.

1 serving: 54 Calories; 3.6 g Total Fat (2.5 g Mono, 0.4 g Poly, 0.5 g Sat); 0 mg Cholesterol; **5 g Carbohydrate**; 2 g Fibre; 2 g Protein; 299 mg Sodium

Mashed Cauliflower

A hint of nutmeg in cheesy cauliflower—yum! Great served with roast beef. Add milk to desired consistency for a delicious soup!

Cauliflower florets	**6 cups**	**1.5 L**
Water		
Grated Parmesan cheese	**1/3 cup**	**75 mL**
Light sour cream	**1/4 cup**	**60 mL**
Hard margarine (or butter), softened	**2 tbsp.**	**30 mL**
Ground nutmeg	**1/4 tsp.**	**1 mL**
Salt	**1/4 tsp.**	**1 mL**

Cook cauliflower in water in large saucepan on medium until tender. Drain. Mash.

Add remaining 5 ingredients. Mix until margarine is melted. Serves 6.

1 serving: 97 Calories; 6.6 g Total Fat (3.5 g Mono, 0.6 g Poly, 2.9 g Sat); 7 mg Cholesterol; **6 g Carbohydrate**; 2 g Fibre; 5 g Protein; 289 mg Sodium

CREAMY CAULIFLOWER: Transfer cooked and cooled cauliflower to blender or food processor. Add remaining 5 ingredients. Process, scraping sides if necessary, until smooth.

Chili Herb Onions

Sweet, golden onions with fragrant herbs and a pleasant chili heat. A great addition to any meat dish.

Canola oil	1 tbsp.	15 mL
Hard margarine (or butter)	1 tbsp.	15 mL
Thinly sliced onion	3 cups	750 mL
Chopped fresh mint leaves (or 3/4 tsp., 4 mL, dried)	1 tbsp.	15 mL
Chopped fresh basil (or 3/4 tsp., 4 mL, dried)	1 tbsp.	15 mL
Low-calorie sweetener (Splenda), or granulated sugar	2 tsp.	10 mL
Dried crushed chilies	1 tsp.	5 mL
Balsamic vinegar	1 tsp.	5 mL
Salt	1/4 tsp.	1 mL

Heat canola oil and margarine in large frying pan on medium-low until margarine is melted. Add onion. Cook for about 20 minutes, stirring often, until caramelized.

Add remaining 6 ingredients. Heat and stir for 1 to 2 minutes to blend flavours. Serves 4.

1 serving: 107 Calories; 6.7 g Total Fat (4 g Mono, 1.4 g Poly, 0.9 g Sat); 0 mg Cholesterol; **11 g Carbohydrate**; 2 g Fibre; 2 g Protein; 193 mg Sodium

Sesame Beans

Glistening sweet-and-sour sauce and a sprinkling of sesame seeds make green beans a new treat!

Canola oil	1 tbsp.	15 mL
White vinegar	1 tbsp.	15 mL
Low-sodium soy sauce	1 tbsp.	15 mL
Granulated sugar (or low-calorie sweetener, Splenda)	1 tbsp.	15 mL
Sesame seeds, toasted (see Tip, page 24)	1 tbsp.	15 mL
Cut fresh (or frozen, thawed and drained) green beans	3 cups	750 mL

(continued on next page)

Combine first 5 ingredients in medium saucepan. Heat and stir on medium for about 2 minutes until sugar is dissolved.

Add green beans. Stir until coated. Cover. Cook for 5 minutes, without stirring. Remove cover. Cook for about 2 minutes, stirring often, until beans are tender-crisp. Serves 4.

1 serving: 85 Calories; 4.7 g Total Fat (2.5 g Mono, 1.6 g Poly, 0.4 g Sat); 0 mg Cholesterol; **10 g Carbohydrate**; 2 g Fibre; 2 g Protein; 129 mg Sodium

Sesame Bok Choy

Asian-style sauce coats tender-crisp bok choy. A great way to get your veggies!

Low-sodium prepared chicken broth	**1/4 cup**	**60 mL**
Oyster sauce	**1 tbsp.**	**15 mL**
Low-sodium soy sauce	**1 tbsp.**	**15 mL**
Cornstarch	**2 tsp.**	**10 mL**
Sesame oil, for flavour	**1/2 tsp.**	**2 mL**
Canola oil	**1 tbsp.**	**15 mL**
Whole baby bok choy (about 6), trimmed, leaves separated	**1 1/4 lbs.**	**560 g**
Sesame seeds, toasted (see Tip, page 24)	**1 tsp.**	**5 mL**

Combine first 5 ingredients in small bowl. Set aside.

Heat wok or large frying pan on medium-high until hot. Add canola oil. Add bok choy. Stir-fry for about 3 minutes until tender-crisp. Stir broth mixture. Add to bok choy. Stir-fry until bok choy is coated and sauce is boiling and thickened. Transfer to serving dish.

Sprinkle with sesame seeds. Serves 4.

1 serving: 169 Calories; 15.6 g Total Fat (6.8 g Mono, 6.1 g Poly, 2 g Sat); 0 mg Cholesterol; **6 g Carbohydrate**; 1 g Fibre; 2 g Protein; 487 mg Sodium

Side Of Spinach

Popeye would have loved this! Honey mustard adds a sweet finish to dark green, earthy spinach.

Olive (or canola) oil	**1 tbsp.**	**15 mL**
Chopped onion	**1/2 cup**	**125 mL**
Garlic cloves, minced (or 1/2 tsp., 2 mL, powder), optional	**2**	**2**
Light sour cream	**3 tbsp.**	**50 mL**
Honey prepared mustard	**2 tsp.**	**10 mL**
Ground nutmeg	**1/8 – 1/4 tsp.**	**0.5 – 1 mL**
Salt	**1/4 tsp.**	**1 mL**
Pepper	**1/4 tsp.**	**1 mL**
Bag of spinach, stems removed (about 6 cups, 1.5 L, lightly packed)	**10 oz.**	**285 g**

Heat olive oil in large frying pan on medium. Add onion. Cook for 5 to 10 minutes, stirring often, until softened.

Add garlic. Heat and stir for 1 to 2 minutes until fragrant.

Combine next 5 ingredients in small cup. Add to onion mixture. Stir.

Add spinach. Heat and stir until just wilted. Serves 4.

1 serving: 71 Calories; 4.6 g Total Fat (3 g Mono, 0.5 g Poly, 1.5 g Sat); 2 mg Cholesterol; **6 g Carbohydrate**; 2 g Fibre; 3 g Protein; 230 mg Sodium

Brie-Filled Mushrooms

Delightfully decadent! Perfect for company. Try these for something a bit different. Makes an excellent side for your favourite poultry.

Bacon slices, cooked crisp and crumbled	**4**	**4**
Jellied cranberry sauce	**1/4 cup**	**60 mL**
Brie cheese round, cut into 12 equal pieces	**4 oz.**	**125 g**
Extra-large fresh whole white mushrooms (about 2 1/2 inch, 6.4 cm, diameter), stems removed	**12**	**12**
Freshly ground pepper, for garnish		

(continued on next page)

Divide and stuff first 3 ingredients, in order given, into mushroom caps. Arrange in single layer on greased baking sheet. Cook in 400°F (205°C) oven for about 15 minutes until mushrooms are tender and cheese is melted.

Sprinkle with pepper. Makes 12 filled mushrooms. Serves 4.

1 serving: 196 Calories; 12.2 g Total Fat (4 g Mono, 0.8 g Poly, 6.6 g Sat); 37 mg Cholesterol; **12 g Carbohydrate**; 2 g Fibre; 11 g Protein; 307 mg Sodium

Pictured on page 125.

Pesto Portobellos

Garlic and basil are perfect accents for these broiled mushrooms. For a different look, peel the skin from the mushroom caps.

Grated Parmesan cheese	3 tbsp.	50 mL
Basil pesto	2 tbsp.	30 mL
Olive (or canola) oil	2 tsp.	10 mL
Garlic clove, minced (or 1/4 tsp., 1 mL, powder)	1	1
Pepper	1/4 tsp.	1 mL
Portobello mushrooms	4	4

Combine first 5 ingredients in small bowl. Mixture will be thick.

Remove mushroom stems with knife. Remove and discard dark gills with spoon. Arrange mushrooms, stem-side down, on greased baking sheet. Spread about 1 1/2 tbsp. (25 mL) Parmesan cheese mixture on each. Broil about 6 inches (15 cm) from heat in oven for about 10 minutes until mushrooms are softened and cheese mixture is bubbling. Serves 4.

1 serving: 101 Calories; 6.6 g Total Fat (3.8 g Mono, 0.7 g Poly, 1.6 g Sat); 4 mg Cholesterol; **8 g Carbohydrate**; 2 g Fibre; 5 g Protein; 95 mg Sodium

Garlic Broccoli

This dish, seasoned with pungent garlic and Chinese five-spice powder, is quick and easy to prepare. Toasted almonds add flavour and crunch.

Broccoli florets	3 cups	750 mL
Water		
Hard margarine (or butter)	2 tbsp.	30 mL
Garlic cloves, minced (or 1/2 tsp., 2 mL, powder)	2	2
Chinese five-spice powder	1/4 tsp.	1 mL
Hoisin sauce	1 tbsp.	15 mL
Pepper	1/4 tsp.	1 mL
Slivered almonds, toasted (see Tip, page 24)	3 tbsp.	50 mL

Cook broccoli in water in medium saucepan on medium until tender-crisp. Drain. Cover to keep warm.

Melt margarine in large frying pan on medium-low. Add garlic and five-spice powder. Heat and stir for 1 to 2 minutes until fragrant.

Add hoisin sauce and pepper. Stir.

Add broccoli and almonds. Toss gently. Serves 4.

1 serving: 121 Calories; 9.3 g Total Fat (5.9 g Mono, 1.4 g Poly, 1.5 g Sat); 0 mg Cholesterol; **8 g Carbohydrate**; 2 g Fibre; 4 g Protein; 186 mg Sodium

Creamy Green Beans

A tasty side dish that's on the table in just minutes!

Frozen French-style green beans	6 cups	1.5 L
Water		
Hard margarine (or butter)	1 1/2 tsp.	7 mL
Chopped onion	1/4 cup	60 mL
Low-fat mayonnaise	1/2 cup	125 mL
Creamed horseradish	1 tsp.	5 mL
Worcestershire sauce	1/2 tsp.	2 mL

(continued on next page)

Cook green beans in water in medium saucepan on medium until tender-crisp. Drain. Cover to keep warm.

Melt margarine in large frying pan on medium. Add onion. Cook for 5 to 10 minutes, stirring often, until softened. Reduce heat to low.

Add mayonnaise, horseradish and Worcestershire sauce. Heat and stir for about 2 minutes until heated through. Add green beans. Toss gently until coated. Serves 4.

1 serving: 179 Calories; 11.5 g Total Fat (6.6 g Mono, 3.3 g Poly, 1 g Sat); 0 mg Cholesterol; **19 g Carbohydrate**; trace Fibre; 4 g Protein; 240 mg Sodium

Crunchy Salsa

An attractive, chunky salsa that invites you to try it! Serve with grilled meats and seafood.

Medium tomatoes, seeds removed, chopped	3	3
Shelled pumpkin seeds, toasted (see Tip, page 24)	2/3 cup	150 mL
Finely chopped red onion	1/4 cup	60 mL
Lime juice	2 tbsp.	30 mL
Sesame seeds, toasted (see Tip, page 24)	2 tsp.	10 mL
Chopped fresh cilantro or parsley (or 1/2 tsp., 2 mL, dried)	2 tsp.	10 mL
Jalapeño pepper, seeds removed, finely diced (see Tip, below)	1	1
Salt	1/4 tsp.	1 mL

Combine all 8 ingredients in medium bowl. Makes 2 1/3 cups (575 mL) salsa.

1/3 cup (75 mL): 142 Calories; 10.3 g Total Fat (3.2 g Mono, 4.7 g Poly, 1.9 g Sat); 0 mg Cholesterol; **7 g Carbohydrate**; 4 g Fibre; 8 g Protein; 95 mg Sodium

Chilies and hot peppers contain capsaicin in seeds and ribs. Removing seeds and ribs will reduce heat. Wear rubber gloves when handling chilies or peppers and avoid touching your eyes. Wash your hands well afterwards.

Lemon Dill Tomatoes

Tangy vinaigrette and feta cheese make tomatoes a delightful side for dinner. Use tomatoes at the peak of ripeness for best flavour.

Olive (or canola) oil	1 tbsp.	15 mL
Lemon juice	1 tbsp.	15 mL
Chopped fresh dill (or 1/2 tsp., 2 mL, dill weed)	2 tsp.	10 mL
Low-calorie sweetener (Splenda), optional	1/4 tsp.	1 mL
Salt	1/4 tsp.	1 mL
Medium tomatoes, cut into 1/4 inch (6 mm) thick slices	3	3
Crumbled feta cheese (about 1 1/4 oz., 35 g)	1/4 cup	60 mL
Freshly ground pepper, for garnish		

Combine first 5 ingredients in jar with tight-fitting lid. Shake well. Makes about 2 tbsp. (30 mL) dressing.

Arrange tomato slices, slightly overlapping, on serving dish. Scatter cheese over top. Drizzle with dressing.

Sprinkle with pepper. Serves 4.

1 serving: 78 Calories; 5.9 g Total Fat (3.1 g Mono, 0.5 g Poly, 2.1 g Sat); 9 mg Cholesterol; **5 g Carbohydrate**; 1 g Fibre; 2 g Protein; 272 mg Sodium

Pictured on page 108.

Broccoli Pecan Salad

Lots of texture in this crunchy, colourful side salad. Creamy dill dressing is light and refreshing.

Low-fat salad dressing (or mayonnaise)	1/4 cup	60 mL
Light sour cream	1/4 cup	60 mL
Chopped fresh dill (or 1 tsp., 5 mL, dill weed)	4 tsp.	20 mL
Dijon mustard	2 tsp.	10 mL
Broccoli florets	4 cups	1 L
Grated light sharp Cheddar cheese	1 cup	250 mL
Chopped pecans, toasted (see Tip, page 24)	1 cup	250 mL
Dried cranberries	2 tbsp.	30 mL

(continued on next page)

Combine first 4 ingredients in large bowl.

Add remaining 4 ingredients. Toss well. Chill for about 1 hour until cold. Makes about 4 cups (1 L) salad. Serves 6.

1 serving: 261 Calories; 21.7 g Total Fat (11.9 g Mono, 4.5 g Poly, 4.7 g Sat); 14 mg Cholesterol; **11 g Carbohydrate**; 3 g Fibre; 9 g Protein; 256 mg Sodium

Pictured on page 125.

Marinated Mushrooms

Delightfully tender and lightly flavoured with herbs and garlic. Great any time!

Water	2 cups	500 mL
Chopped onion	1/2 cup	125 mL
Lemon juice	1/3 cup	75 mL
Olive (or canola) oil	1/4 cup	60 mL
Whole black peppercorns	1 tbsp.	15 mL
Dried whole oregano	2 tsp.	10 mL
Garlic cloves, minced (or 1/2 tsp., 2 mL, powder)	2	2
Bay leaves	2	2
Salt, just a pinch		
Small fresh whole white mushrooms	2 lbs.	900 g
Chopped fresh parsley	1 tbsp.	15 mL

Combine first 9 ingredients in large pot or Dutch oven. Bring to a boil on medium-high.

Add mushrooms. Cook for 5 minutes, stirring occasionally, to blend flavours. Transfer to large bowl. Cool. Cover. Marinate in refrigerator for at least 6 hours or overnight, stirring occasionally.

Remove mushrooms with slotted spoon to medium bowl. Discard marinade. Sprinkle mushrooms with parsley. May be stored, covered, in refrigerator for up to 5 days. Serves 8.

1 serving: 64 Calories; 3.9 g Total Fat (2.5 g Mono, 0.5 g Poly, 0.5 g Sat); 0 mg Cholesterol; **7 g Carbohydrate**; 2 g Fibre; 3 g Protein; 5 mg Sodium

Pictured on page 125.

Shrimp Chips And Dip

Shrimp chips are a delicious, unusual snack that will have everyone asking how you made them. Roasted garlic dip also goes well with your favourite vegetables.

ROASTED GARLIC DIP

Garlic bulb	1	1
Olive oil	1/2 tsp.	2 mL
Block of light cream cheese, softened	4 oz.	125 g
Low-fat salad dressing (or mayonnaise)	1/4 cup	60 mL
Worcestershire sauce	1/2 tsp.	2 mL
Lemon juice	1/4 tsp.	1 mL

SHRIMP CHIPS

Fresh (or frozen, thawed) uncooked medium shrimp (tails removed), peeled and deveined	8 oz.	225 g
Cornstarch	1 tbsp.	15 mL
Dijon mustard	1 tsp.	5 mL
Garlic clove, minced (or 1/4 tsp., 1 mL, powder)	1	1
Caraway seed	1/2 tsp.	2 mL
Rice paper rounds (8 1/2 inch, 21 cm, diameter)	5	5
Canola oil, for deep-frying		

Roasted Garlic Dip: Remove and discard top 1/4 inch (6 mm) from garlic bulb to expose cloves. Drizzle olive oil over top. Wrap loosely in foil. Bake in 350°F (175°C) oven for 40 to 45 minutes until softened and golden. Cool. Remove and discard foil. Squeeze garlic bulb to remove cloves. Discard peel. Transfer cloves to blender or food processor.

Add next 4 ingredients. Process until smooth. Transfer to medium bowl. Cover. Chill for at least 1 hour to blend flavours. Makes about 1 cup (250 mL) dip.

Shrimp Chips: Process first 5 ingredients in blender or food processor until smooth.

Spread about 2 tbsp. (30 mL) shrimp mixture evenly on 1 rice paper round. Cut round into 12 wedges. Repeat with remaining shrimp mixture and rice paper rounds. Deep-fry in 8 batches, shrimp-side down, in hot (375°F, 190°C) canola oil for 1 to 1 1/2 minutes, turning once, until golden. Remove each batch to paper towels to drain. Makes 60 shrimp chips. Serve with Roasted Garlic Dip. Serves 6.

1 serving: 247 Calories; 19.3 g Total Fat (10 g Mono, 4.6 g Poly, 3.5 g Sat); 56 mg Cholesterol; **10 g Carbohydrate**; trace Fibre; 9 g Protein; 287 mg Sodium

Gouda Crisps

These look like lace cookies. Pretty on a tray of finger food. Make these with any firm cheese, such as Cheddar, Swiss or Gruyère.

Grated Gouda cheese	1/2 cup	125 mL

Divide cheese into 4 equal portions. Arrange portions, evenly spaced apart, on parchment paper-lined baking sheet. Loosely spread each portion into 4 inch (10 cm) diameter round. Bake in 425°F (220°C) oven for 8 to 10 minutes until edges are golden and cheese is bubbling. Let stand on baking sheet on wire rack until cool. Store in airtight container for up to 2 days. Makes 4 crisps.

1 crisp: 63 Calories; 4.9 g Total Fat (1.4 g Mono, 0.1 g Poly, 3.1 g Sat); 20 mg Cholesterol; **0 g Carbohydrate**; 0 g Fibre; 4 g Protein; 146 mg Sodium

GOUDA CARAWAY CRISPS: Sprinkle Gouda cheese with caraway seed before baking.

CHEDDAR PEPPER CRISPS: Omit Gouda cheese. Use same amount of Cheddar cheese and sprinkle with pepper before baking.

Stuffed Celery Nibbles

A crunchy, casual snack. Horseradish adds zip!

Block of light cream cheese, softened	4 oz.	125 g
Finely chopped water chestnuts, optional	2 tbsp.	30 mL
Creamed horseradish	1 tbsp.	15 mL
Paprika	2 tsp.	10 mL
Grated light sharp Cheddar cheese	1 cup	250 mL
Celery ribs (3 inches, 7.5 cm, each)	24	24

Combine first 4 ingredients in medium bowl.

Add Cheddar cheese. Stir until just combined. Spread about 2 tsp. (10 mL) cheese mixture in 1 celery rib. Repeat with remaining cheese mixture and celery ribs. Serves 6.

1 serving: 119 Calories; 8.2 g Total Fat (2.5 g Mono, 0.3 g Poly, 4.9 g Sat); 25 mg Cholesterol; **4 g Carbohydrate**; 1 g Fibre; 7 g Protein; 322 mg Sodium

Almond Cheese

An appetizing cheese roll with a peppery personality. Almonds add crunch.

Grated light sharp Cheddar cheese	1 cup	250 mL
Block of light cream cheese, softened	4 oz.	125 g
Chopped fresh parsley (or 1 1/2 tsp., 7 mL, flakes)	2 tbsp.	30 mL
Dry sherry	1 tbsp.	15 mL
Dijon mustard (with whole seeds)	1 tsp.	5 mL
Cayenne pepper	1/4 tsp.	1 mL
Sliced almonds, toasted (see Tip, page 24)	1/3 cup	75 mL

Combine first 6 ingredients in small bowl. Roll into 6 inch (15 cm) long log.

Roll log in almonds in small shallow dish until coated. Wrap in waxed paper. Chill for about 3 hours until firm. Cuts into twenty-four 1/4 inch (6 mm) slices. Serves 8.

1 serving: 110 Calories; 8.5 g Total Fat (3.4 g Mono, 0.7 g Poly, 3.9 g Sat); 19 mg Cholesterol; **2 g Carbohydrate**; trace Fibre; 6 g Protein; 215 mg Sodium

Herbed Mozzarella

Mild mozzarella becomes a tangy treat with this delicious marinade! Serve cheese cubes on cocktail picks for an attractive presentation.

HERB MARINADE		
Canola oil	1/3 cup	75 mL
Chopped fresh parsley (or 3/4 tsp., 4 mL, flakes)	1 tbsp.	15 mL
Finely chopped sun-dried tomatoes in oil, drained (oil reserved)	1 tbsp.	15 mL
Reserved sun-dried tomato oil	2 tsp.	10 mL
Chopped fresh basil (or 1/2 tsp., 2 mL, dried)	2 tsp.	10 mL
Chopped fresh chives (or 1/4 tsp., 1 mL, dried)	1 tsp.	5 mL
Garlic clove, minced (or 1/4 tsp., 1 mL, powder)	1	1
Dried crushed chilies	1/4 tsp.	1 mL
Part-skim mozzarella cheese, cut into 1/2 inch (12 mm) cubes	1 lb.	454 g

(continued on next page)

Herb Marinade: Combine first 8 ingredients in medium bowl. Makes about 1/3 cup (75 mL) marinade.

Add cheese cubes. Stir until coated. Marinate in refrigerator for at least 6 hours or overnight, stirring occasionally. Remove cheese with slotted spoon to large plate. Discard marinade. Serves 8.

1 serving: 162 Calories; 10.5 g Total Fat (3.3 g Mono, 0.6 g Poly, 6 g Sat); 34 mg Cholesterol; **2 g Carbohydrate**; trace Fibre; 14 g Protein; 279 mg Sodium

Pictured on page 126.

Spicy Sweet Drumettes

These won't last long! Make sure you have plenty of napkins or finger bowls available for sticky fingers.

SWEET AND SPICY MARINADE

Low-sodium soy sauce	3 tbsp.	50 mL
Worcestershire sauce	2 tbsp.	30 mL
Brown sugar, packed	2 tbsp.	30 mL
Dried crushed chilies	1 – 2 tsp.	5 – 10 mL
Ground coriander	1 tsp.	5 mL
Ground ginger	1 tsp.	5 mL
Garlic salt	1/2 tsp.	2 mL
Chicken drumettes (about 16), skin removed	2 lbs.	900 g

Sweet And Spicy Marinade: Combine first 7 ingredients in large bowl. Makes about 1/3 cup (75 mL) marinade.

Add drumettes. Turn until coated. Cover. Marinate in refrigerator for at least 6 hours or overnight, stirring once. Arrange drumettes in single layer on greased wire rack set in greased baking sheet with sides. Cook in 375°F (190°C) oven for 15 minutes. Brush drumettes with remaining marinade. Cook for about 40 minutes until chicken is no longer pink. Makes about 16 drumettes. Serves 4.

1 serving: 188 Calories; 4.3 g Total Fat (1.1 g Mono, 1 g Poly, 1.1 g Sat); 66 mg Cholesterol; **9 g Carbohydrate**; trace Fibre; 27 g Protein; 711 mg Sodium

Creamy Avocado Dip

Smooth, creamy and delicious—you won't be able to stop eating this one once you start! Serve with low-carb vegetables.

Ripe large avocados, chopped	**2**	**2**
Light sour cream	**1/4 cup**	**60 mL**
Finely chopped red onion	**1/4 cup**	**60 mL**
Lemon (or lime) juice	**1 tbsp.**	**15 mL**
Sweet chili sauce	**1 1/2 tsp.**	**7 mL**
Garlic powder	**1/8 tsp.**	**0.5 mL**
Salt, just a pinch		
Pepper, sprinkle		

Mash avocado in medium bowl until smooth.

Add remaining 7 ingredients. Stir well. Cover. Chill for 1 hour to blend flavours. Makes about 1 2/3 cups (400 mL) dip.

2 tbsp. (30 mL): 56 Calories; 5.1 g Total Fat (3.2 g Mono, 0.6 g Poly, 1.2 g Sat); 1 mg Cholesterol; **3 g Carbohydrate**; 1 g Fibre; 1 g Protein; 14 mg Sodium

1. Marinated Mushrooms, page 119
2. Broccoli Pecan Salad, page 118
3. Brie-Filled Mushrooms, page 114

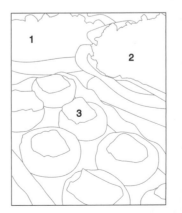

Spicy Nuts

Crunchy and flavoured with curry—sure to satisfy any craving!

Cashews	1 cup	250 mL
Pecan halves	1 cup	250 mL
Shelled pumpkin seeds	1/2 cup	125 mL
Hard margarine (or butter), melted	2 tbsp.	30 mL
Egg white (large)	1	1
Curry powder	2 tsp.	10 mL
Salt	1/2 tsp.	2 mL
Cayenne pepper	1/4 tsp.	1 mL

Scatter cashews, pecans and pumpkin seeds in 3 quart (3 L) shallow baking dish. Drizzle margarine over top. Stir until coated. Spread evenly. Bake in 350°F (175°C) oven for 8 to 10 minutes, stirring occasionally, until lightly toasted. Let stand for 5 minutes.

Beat egg white in small bowl until soft peaks form. Add remaining 3 ingredients. Beat well. Add to nut mixture. Stir until coated. Spread evenly. Bake in 275°F (140°C) oven for about 30 minutes, stirring twice, until mixture is dry and cashews are golden. Makes 2 1/2 cups (625 mL) nuts.

1/4 cup (60 mL): 246 Calories; 21.9 g Total Fat (11.8 g Mono, 5.6 g Poly, 3.4 g Sat); 0 mg Cholesterol; **9 g Carbohydrate**; 3 g Fibre; 7 g Protein; 156 mg Sodium

Pictured on page 126.

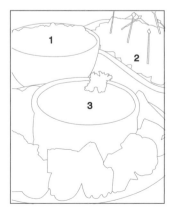

1. Spicy Nuts, above
2. Herbed Mozzarella, page 122
3. Chili Con Queso Dip, page 130

Herb Pepper Pork Pâté

Serve this flavourful meat spread on thin low-carb crackers or cucumber slices. Garnish with chopped fresh chives or parsley.

Finely chopped onion	**1 1/2 cups**	**375 mL**
Dry white (or alcohol-free) wine (or low-sodium prepared chicken broth)	**3/4 cup**	**175 mL**
Garlic cloves, minced	**7**	**7**
Dried thyme	**1 1/2 tsp.**	**7 mL**
Bay leaves	**2**	**2**
Dried whole oregano	**1/4 tsp.**	**1 mL**
Ground allspice	**1/4 tsp.**	**1 mL**
Salt	**1 tsp.**	**5 mL**
Coarse ground pepper	**1 tsp.**	**5 mL**
Boneless pork shoulder butt steaks (or roast), cut into 1 inch (2.5 cm) pieces	**1 1/4 lbs.**	**560 g**

Combine first 9 ingredients in large saucepan.

Add pork. Stir. Bring to a boil on medium-high. Reduce heat to medium-low. Cover. Simmer for about 1 hour until pork is tender. Drain, reserving 1 cup (250 mL) liquid from saucepan in small bowl. Let stand for 5 minutes. Discard remaining liquid and bay leaves. Process pork and reserved liquid, in 2 batches, in blender or food processor until smooth. Spread mixture evenly in 1 quart (1 L) casserole. Cover. Chill overnight. Store, covered, in refrigerator for up to 1 week. Makes about 3 1/4 cups (800 mL) pâté.

2 tbsp. (30 mL): 68 Calories; 4.3 g Total Fat (1.9 g Mono, 0.5 g Poly, 1.5 g Sat); 14 mg Cholesterol; **1 g Carbohydrate**; trace Fibre; 4 g Protein; 115 mg Sodium

Mustard Chicken Strips

Wrap these in lettuce leaves, or serve with your favourite dip. Nutty and sweet.

HONEY MUSTARD MARINADE

Dijon mustard	2 tbsp.	30 mL
Liquid honey	2 tsp.	10 mL
Low-sodium soy sauce	2 tsp.	10 mL
Apple cider vinegar	2 tsp.	10 mL
Drops of hot pepper sauce	2 – 3	2 – 3
Boneless, skinless chicken breast halves (about 2), each cut lengthwise into 8 strips	1/2 lb.	225 g
Large egg	1	1
Milk	2 tbsp.	30 mL
Ground pecans, toasted (see Tip, page 24)	1/3 cup	75 mL
Fine dry bread crumbs	2 tbsp.	30 mL
Dried whole oregano	1/2 tsp.	2 mL
Canola oil	2 tbsp.	30 mL

Honey Mustard Marinade: Combine first 5 ingredients in small bowl. Makes about 1/4 cup (60 mL) marinade.

Put chicken strips into medium resealable freezer bag. Pour marinade over top. Seal bag. Turn until coated. Marinate in refrigerator for at least 6 hours or overnight, turning occasionally. Drain and discard marinade.

Beat egg and milk with fork in small shallow dish until well combined.

Combine pecans, bread crumbs and oregano in separate small shallow dish. Dip each chicken strip into egg mixture. Press both sides of each strip in pecan mixture until coated.

Heat canola oil in large frying pan on medium. Add chicken strips. Cook for about 3 minutes per side until chicken is no longer pink inside. Makes 16 chicken strips. Serves 4.

1 serving: 240 Calories; 16.7 g Total Fat (9.2 g Mono, 4.4 g Poly, 1.8 g Sat); 95 mg Cholesterol; **4 g Carbohydrate**; trace Fibre; 19 g Protein; 115 mg Sodium

Chili Con Queso Dip

This chil-lee cahn KAY-soh dip is perfect for fresh vegetables or Belgian endive leaves. Serve warm.

Canola oil	1/2 tsp.	2 mL
Finely chopped onion	1/2 cup	125 mL
Finely diced fresh green chili (or jalapeño) pepper (see Tip, page 117)	1 tbsp.	15 mL
Grated light sharp Cheddar cheese	4 cups	1 L
Diced tomatoes (with juice)	1/2 cup	125 mL
Dried crushed chilies	1/2 tsp.	2 mL
Garlic powder	1/4 tsp.	1 mL

Heat canola oil in large saucepan on medium. Add onion and chili pepper. Cook for 5 to 10 minutes, stirring often, until onion is softened.

Add remaining 4 ingredients. Heat and stir until heated through and cheese is melted. Makes about 1 1/2 cups (375 mL) dip.

2 tbsp. (30 mL): 129 Calories; 8.2 g Total Fat (2.5 g Mono, 0.2 g Poly, 5.1 g Sat); 24 mg Cholesterol; **2 g Carbohydrate**; trace Fibre; 10 g Protein; 257 mg Sodium

Pictured on page 126.

Sun-Dried Tomato Dip

This tangy, creamy dip is a great addition to a tray of vegetables.

Light sour cream	1/2 cup	125 mL
Low-fat salad dressing (or mayonnaise)	1/2 cup	125 mL
Sun-dried tomatoes in oil, drained, cut up	1/3 cup	75 mL
Chopped fresh basil (or 3/4 tsp., 4 mL, dried)	1 tbsp.	15 mL
Garlic clove, minced (or 1/4 tsp., 1 mL, powder), optional	1	1
Pepper	1/4 tsp.	1 mL

Process all 6 ingredients in blender or food processor, scraping down sides if necessary, until smooth. Transfer to small bowl. Cover. Chill for 1 to 2 hours to blend flavours. Makes about 1 1/4 cups (300 mL) dip.

2 tbsp. (30 mL): 55 Calories; 4.6 g Total Fat (2.7 g Mono, 1.1 g Poly, 1.3 g Sat); 2 mg Cholesterol; **3 g Carbohydrate**; 0 g Fibre; 1 g Protein; 111 mg Sodium

Nutty Blue Cheese

Creamy blue cheese coated with parsley and crunchy walnuts. An elegant addition to any party tray.

Block of light cream cheese, softened	8 oz.	250 g
Crumbled blue cheese (about 3 1/2 oz., 100 g)	1 1/3 cups	325 mL
Finely chopped walnuts	1/4 cup	60 mL
Onion powder	1 tsp.	5 mL
Garlic powder	1 tsp.	5 mL
Creamed horseradish	1 tsp.	5 mL
Finely chopped walnuts, toasted (see Tip, page 24)	1/4 cup	60 mL
Chopped fresh parsley	2 tbsp.	30 mL
Belgian endive leaves	20	20
Celery ribs (3 inches, 7.5 cm, each)	30	30

Combine first 6 ingredients in medium bowl. Cover. Chill for 1 hour to blend flavours. Shape cream cheese mixture into ball.

Combine second amount of walnuts and parsley in medium shallow dish. Roll cheese ball in walnut mixture until coated. Makes about 1 2/3 cups (400 mL). Place cheese ball on large serving dish.

Arrange endive leaves and celery pieces around cheese ball. Serves 10.

1 serving: 142 Calories; 11.6 g Total Fat (3.1 g Mono, 2.8 g Poly, 4.9 g Sat); 23 mg Cholesterol; **4 g Carbohydrate**; 1 g Fibre; 7 g Protein; 350 mg Sodium

Bacon Dip

A thick, savoury dip everyone will love. Serve with a variety of fresh vegetables.

Light sour cream	1 cup	250 mL
Bacon slices, cooked crisp and crumbled	4	4
Ranch-style dressing	3 tbsp.	50 mL
Finely sliced green onion	3 tbsp.	50 mL
Garlic clove, minced (or 1/4 tsp., 1 mL, powder)	1	1
Pepper	1/4 tsp.	1 mL

Combine all 6 ingredients in medium bowl. Chill for 2 to 3 hours to blend flavours. Makes about 1 1/3 cups (325 mL) dip.

2 tbsp. (30 mL): 53 Calories; 4.7 g Total Fat (1.4 g Mono, 0.3 g Poly, 2.7 g Sat); 8 mg Cholesterol; **1 g Carbohydrate**; trace Fibre; 2 g Protein; 87 mg Sodium

Dry Ribs

These crisp, tasty morsels are tender and chewy.

Sweet and sour cut pork ribs, trimmed of fat, cut into 1-bone portions	**2 lbs.**	**900 g**
Water		
Low-sodium soy sauce	**2 tbsp.**	**30 mL**
Dry sherry	**2 tbsp.**	**30 mL**
Green onions, minced	**2**	**2**
Garlic clove, minced (or 1/4 tsp., 1 mL, powder)	**1**	**1**
Finely grated, peeled gingerroot	**1/2 tsp.**	**2 mL**
Egg whites (large)	**2**	**2**
Water	**1 tbsp.**	**15 mL**
Cornstarch	**1/4 cup**	**60 mL**
Canola oil, for deep-frying		
Salt	**1 tsp.**	**5 mL**

Put ribs into large pot or Dutch oven. Add enough water to cover. Bring to a boil on medium-high. Reduce heat to medium. Cover. Simmer for about 20 minutes until pork is just tender. Drain. Cool. Blot dry with paper towels.

Combine next 5 ingredients in large bowl. Add ribs. Stir until coated. Cover. Marinate in refrigerator for 1 to 4 hours, stirring occasionally. Drain and discard marinade.

Combine egg whites, second amount of water and cornstarch in separate large bowl. Add ribs. Stir until coated.

Deep-fry ribs, in 2 batches, in hot (375°F, 190°C) canola oil for 2 to 3 minutes per batch until browned. Remove with slotted spoon to paper towels to drain. While still hot, sprinkle each batch with 1/2 tsp. (2 mL) salt. Makes about 60 ribs. Serves 10.

1 serving: 248 Calories; 19.7 g Total Fat (9.7 g Mono, 3.4 g Poly, 5.1 g Sat); 46 mg Cholesterol; **3 g Carbohydrate**; trace Fibre; 13 g Protein; 348 mg Sodium

Chocolate Popcorn

Crunchy, chocolate-coated popcorn is delightful!

Bag of butter-flavoured microwave popcorn	3 1/2 oz.	99 g
Semi-sweet chocolate baking squares (1 oz., 28 g, each), chopped	3	3

Prepare popcorn according to package directions. Spread popcorn evenly on waxed paper-lined baking sheet. Set aside.

Heat chocolate in small heavy saucepan on lowest heat, stirring often, until almost melted (see Note). Do not overheat. Remove from heat. Stir until smooth. Drizzle over popcorn. Toss gently until coated. Chill for about 30 minutes until set. Makes about 10 1/2 cups (2.6 L) popcorn.

1 cup (250 mL): 86 Calories; 5.1 g Total Fat (1.6 g Mono, 1.4 g Poly, 2 g Sat); 0 mg Cholesterol; **11 g Carbohydrate**; 1 g Fibre; 1 g Protein; 85 mg Sodium

Pictured on page 143.

Note: Chocolate can be melted in microwave. Heat chocolate in small dish in microwave on medium (50%) for 2 to 3 minutes, stirring occasionally, until smooth.

Tropical Treats

Little snowballs of creamy coconut and pineapple are a refreshing sweet snack.

Pineapple spreadable cream cheese, softened	7 oz.	200 g
Frozen whipped topping, thawed	1/2 cup	125 mL
Medium sweetened coconut, toasted (see Tip, page 24)	1/2 cup	125 mL
Coconut flavouring	1/8 tsp.	0.5 mL

Combine all 4 ingredients in medium bowl. Use 1 1/4 inch (3 cm) scoop to drop mounds, evenly spaced apart, onto waxed paper-lined baking sheet. Cover. Freeze for about 2 hours until firm. Store in airtight container in freezer. Makes about 2 dozen (24) treats.

1 treat: 42 Calories; 3.9 g Total Fat (0.9 g Mono, 0.1 g Poly, 2.7 g Sat); 9 mg Cholesterol; **1 g Carbohydrate**; trace Fibre; 1 g Protein; 29 mg Sodium

Chewy Coconut Cookies

Chewy coconut and crunchy almonds make these citrus-kissed cookies a great light snack.

Flake coconut	2 cups	500 mL
Low-calorie sweetener (Splenda)	1/2 cup	125 mL
Milk	1/2 cup	125 mL
Light sour cream	1/2 cup	125 mL
Block of light cream cheese, softened	4 oz.	125 g
Large eggs	2	2
Sliced almonds, toasted (see Tip, page 24)	2/3 cup	150 mL
Lemon zest	1 tsp.	5 mL
Orange zest	1 tsp.	5 mL

Combine first 4 ingredients in medium bowl. Chill for 1 hour.

Beat cream cheese and eggs in large bowl until smooth. Add coconut mixture and remaining 3 ingredients. Stir. Drop, using 1 tbsp. (15 mL) for each, about 2 inches (5 cm) apart onto parchment paper-lined cookie sheets. Bake in 350°F (175°C) oven for about 15 minutes until golden. Let stand on cookie sheets for 5 minutes before removing to wire racks to cool. Makes about 2 dozen (24) cookies.

1 cookie: 97 Calories; 8.6 g Total Fat (2 g Mono, 0.5 g Poly, 5.9 g Sat); 22 mg Cholesterol; **3 g Carbohydrate**; 1 g Fibre; 3 g Protein; 50 mg Sodium

Sweet Spiced Nuts

Subtle sweetness and a nice blend of spices make these hard to resist!

Low-calorie sweetener (Splenda)	1/3 cup	75 mL
Egg white (large)	1	1
Water	1 tbsp.	15 mL
Ground cinnamon	1/2 tsp.	2 mL
Ground ginger	1/4 tsp.	1 mL
Ground nutmeg	1/4 tsp.	1 mL
Salt	1/4 tsp.	1 mL
Pecan halves	1 cup	250 mL
Shelled pistachios	1 cup	250 mL
Whole natural almonds	1 cup	250 mL

(continued on next page)

Beat first 7 ingredients in large bowl until frothy.

Add remaining 3 ingredients. Stir until coated. Spread evenly on parchment paper-lined baking sheet with sides. Bake in 275°F (140°C) oven for about 45 minutes, stirring occasionally, until crisp and golden. Cool. Store in airtight container for up to 2 weeks. Makes 3 cups (750 mL) nuts.

1/4 cup (60 mL): 210 Calories; 18.9 g Total Fat (12.3 g Mono, 3.9 g Poly, 1.9 g Sat); 0 mg Cholesterol; **8 g Carbohydrate**; 2 g Fibre; 5 g Protein; 56 mg Sodium

Creamy Lime Freezies

Creamy pudding popsicles the whole family will love. Use a popsicle mold, if you have one.

Boiling water	1 cup	250 mL
Box of light lime-flavoured jelly powder (gelatin), 4 serving size	1	1
Non-fat vanilla yogurt	1 cup	250 mL
Paper cups (5 oz., 142 mL, size)	4	4
Wooden popsicle sticks	4	4

Pour boiling water into 4 cup (1 L) liquid measure. Add jelly powder. Stir until dissolved. Let stand for 10 minutes.

Add yogurt. Stir.

Divide and pour yogurt mixture into paper cups until 3/4 full. Cover top of each cup with foil. Cut small slit in centre of each piece of foil. Insert 1 popsicle stick through each slit to bottom of each cup. Freeze overnight until firm. Run each cup under hot water for 3 to 4 seconds to loosen freezies. Remove and discard cups. Makes 4 freezies.

1 freezie: 106 Calories; 0.1 g Total Fat (0 g Mono, 0 g Poly, 0 g Sat); 1 mg Cholesterol; **12 g Carbohydrate**; 0 g Fibre; 15 g Protein; 506 mg Sodium

Variation: Use a combination of your favourite flavours of jelly powder and yogurt to make other flavoured freezies.

Nutty Granola

Crunchy nut and apple combination. Try it with milk for breakfast.

Chopped pecans	**1/2 cup**	**125 mL**
Walnut pieces	**1/2 cup**	**125 mL**
Sliced almonds	**1/2 cup**	**125 mL**
Medium unsweetened coconut	**1/2 cup**	**125 mL**
Shelled sunflower seeds	**1/2 cup**	**125 mL**
Hard margarine (or butter), melted	**1/4 cup**	**60 mL**
Low-calorie sweetener (Splenda)	**1/4 cup**	**60 mL**
Ground cinnamon	**1 tsp.**	**5 mL**
Vanilla	**1/2 tsp.**	**2 mL**
Chopped dried apple	**3/4 cup**	**175 mL**

Combine first 5 ingredients in large bowl.

Measure next 4 ingredients into small bowl. Stir well. Drizzle over nut mixture. Toss until coated. Spread evenly in ungreased baking sheet with sides. Bake in 350°F (175°C) oven for about 10 minutes, stirring once, until golden. Cool.

Add apple. Stir. Store in airtight container for up to 1 month. Makes about 3 1/4 cups (800 mL) granola.

1/4 cup (60 mL): 190 Calories; 17 g Total Fat (7.1 g Mono, 5.4 g Poly, 3.7 g Sat); 0 mg Cholesterol; **8 g Carbohydrate**; 2 g Fibre; 4 g Protein; 49 mg Sodium

Pictured on page 143.

Cream Kisses

Keep these mocha-coloured, creamy "kisses" in the freezer for those times when you want something sweet.

Whipping cream	**1 cup**	**250 mL**
Block of light cream cheese, softened	**8 oz.**	**250 g**
Box of fat-free instant chocolate pudding powder (4 serving size)	**1**	**1**
Milk	**1/4 cup**	**60 mL**
Light sour cream	**2 tbsp.**	**30 mL**

(continued on next page)

Beat whipping cream in small bowl until soft peaks form. Set aside.

Beat remaining 4 ingredients in large bowl until smooth. Fold in whipped cream. Spoon cream cheese mixture into piping bag fitted with large star tip. Pipe about thirty-six 1 to 1 1/2 inch (2.5 to 3.8 cm) diameter mounds, evenly spaced apart, onto waxed paper-lined baking sheets. Freeze for about 1 hour until firm. Store in airtight container in freezer. Makes about 3 dozen (36) cream kisses.

1 cream kiss: 49 Calories; 3.7 g Total Fat (1.1 g Mono, 0.1 g Poly, 2.3 g Sat); 13 mg Cholesterol; **3 g Carbohydrate**; 0 g Fibre; 1 g Protein; 97 mg Sodium

Variation: Omit chocolate pudding powder. Use your favourite pudding flavour.

Peanut Pecan Cookies

Crunchy, delicate cookies. No flour in these!

Brown sugar, packed	1/2 cup	125 mL
Baking powder	1/4 tsp.	1 mL
Crunchy peanut butter	1 cup	250 mL
Large egg	1	1
Finely chopped pecans	1/4 cup	60 mL

Combine brown sugar and baking powder in medium bowl. Add peanut butter. Beat until smooth. Add egg. Beat well.

Add pecans. Stir. Roll dough into 1 inch (2.5 cm) balls. Arrange balls, about 1 1/2 inches (3.8 cm) apart, on ungreased cookie sheets. Flatten with fork. Bake in 325°F (160°C) oven for about 8 minutes until tops are set. Let stand on cookie sheets for 5 minutes before removing to wire racks to cool. Makes about 3 dozen (36) cookies.

1 cookie: 65 Calories; 4.5 g Total Fat (2.2 g Mono, 1.3 g Poly, 0.8 g Sat); 6 mg Cholesterol; **5 g Carbohydrate**; 1 g Fibre; 2 g Protein; 42 mg Sodium

Chocolate Cups

A creamy dessert "choc-full" of good taste! This may be made and served in individual ramekins.

Envelope of unflavoured gelatin	1/4 oz.	7 g
Water	1/4 cup	60 mL
Whipping cream	1/4 cup	60 mL
Block of light cream cheese, cut up	8 oz.	250 g
Semi-sweet chocolate baking squares	4	4
(1 oz., 28 g, each), chopped		
Low-calorie sweetener (Splenda)	1/2 cup	125 mL
Vanilla	1 tsp.	5 mL
Whipping cream	3/4 cup	175 mL
Pecan halves, toasted (see Tip, page 24)	8	8

Sprinkle gelatin over water in small saucepan. Let stand for 1 minute. Heat and stir on low until gelatin is dissolved. Remove from heat. Let stand for 5 minutes.

Heat first amount of whipping cream in separate small saucepan on medium-low for about 5 minutes until bubbles form around edge.

Add cream cheese and chocolate. Heat and stir for about 5 minutes until smooth. Pour into large heatproof bowl.

Add gelatin mixture, sweetener and vanilla. Stir well. Cool until syrupy.

Beat second amount of whipping cream in small bowl until stiff peaks form. Fold into chocolate mixture. Line each of 8 muffin cups with plastic wrap. Divide and spoon chocolate mixture evenly into each. Chill for about 2 hours until set. Holding plastic wrap, carefully lift each chocolate cup from muffin pan. Invert chocolate cups onto 8 individual plates. Remove and discard plastic wrap.

Place 1 pecan half on top of each chocolate cup. Serves 8.

1 serving: 256 Calories; 21.6 g Total Fat (7 g Mono, 1 g Poly, 12.4 g Sat); 56 mg Cholesterol; **11 g Carbohydrate**; 1 g Fibre; 5 g Protein; 233 mg Sodium

Chocolate Cheesecake

A dark, hazelnut crust lies beneath creamy cheesecake drizzled with chocolate.

CHOCOLATE HAZELNUT CRUST		
Ground hazelnuts (filberts)	1 cup	250 mL
Hard margarine (or butter), melted	3 tbsp.	50 mL
Cocoa, sifted if lumpy	3 tbsp.	50 mL
Low-calorie sweetener (Splenda)	2 tbsp.	30 mL
LIGHT CREAM CHEESE FILLING		
Blocks of light cream cheese (8 oz., 250 g, each), softened	2	2
Light sour cream	1 cup	250 mL
Low-calorie sweetener (Splenda)	1/2 cup	125 mL
Large eggs	3	3
Semi-sweet chocolate baking squares (1 oz., 28 g, each)	2	2
Hard margarine (or butter)	2 tsp.	10 mL

Chocolate Hazelnut Crust: Combine all 4 ingredients in small bowl. Press firmly in bottom of greased 8 inch (20 cm) springform pan. Bake in 350°F (175°C) oven for 10 minutes. Cool completely.

Light Cream Cheese Filling: Beat cream cheese, sour cream and sweetener in medium bowl until smooth. Add eggs, 1 at a time, beating after each addition until just combined. Spread evenly over crust. Bake in 325°F (160°C) oven for about 50 minutes until centre is almost set. Remove from oven. Run knife around inside edge of pan to allow cheesecake to settle evenly. Let stand in pan on wire rack until cooled completely.

Heat chocolate and margarine in small heavy saucepan on lowest heat, stirring often, until chocolate is almost melted. Do not overheat. Remove from heat. Stir until smooth. Drizzle over cheesecake. Chill for at least 6 hours or overnight. Cuts into 12 wedges.

1 wedge: 256 Calories; 22.2 g Total Fat (11.6 g Mono, 1.6 g Poly, 8.9 g Sat); 84 mg Cholesterol; **8 g Carbohydrate**; 1 g Fibre; 8 g Protein; 357 mg Sodium

Chocolate Pear Crêpes

A light dessert with fluffy chocolate filling and a drizzle of rich pear sauce.

ALMOND CRÊPES

Milk	2/3 cup	150 mL
Ground almonds	1/4 cup	60 mL
Large eggs	3	3
All-purpose flour	3 tbsp.	50 mL
Hard margarine (or butter), melted	2 tbsp.	30 mL
Low-calorie sweetener (Splenda)	1 tbsp.	15 mL
Salt	1/4 tsp.	1 mL
Canola oil	2 tsp.	10 mL

CHOCOLATE PEAR FILLING

Whipping cream	1 cup	250 mL
Low-calorie sweetener (Splenda)	2 tbsp.	30 mL
Cocoa, sifted if lumpy	1 tbsp.	15 mL
Vanilla	1/2 tsp.	2 mL
Can of pear halves, drained (juice reserved), blotted dry and sliced	14 oz.	398 mL

PEAR SAUCE

Unflavoured gelatin	1/2 tsp.	2 mL
Reserved juice from pear halves	3/4 cup	175 mL
Hard margarine (or butter), softened	2 tbsp.	30 mL
Low-calorie sweetener (Splenda)	1 tbsp.	15 mL

Almond Crêpes: Beat first 7 ingredients in small bowl until smooth. Cover. Chill for 1 hour. Makes about 1 2/3 cups (400 mL) batter.

Heat 1/4 tsp. (1 mL) canola oil in 8 inch (20 cm) non-stick frying pan on medium. Stir batter. Measure 3 tbsp. (50 mL) batter into 1/4 cup (60 mL) measure. Pour into pan. Immediately swirl pan to coat bottom, lifting and tilting pan to ensure entire bottom is covered. Cook for 1 to 1 1/2 minutes until top is set. Turn. Cook for about 30 seconds until brown spots appear on bottom. Remove to medium plate. Repeat with remaining canola oil and batter. Makes 8 crêpes.

Chocolate Pear Filling: Beat first 4 ingredients in medium bowl until stiff peaks form.

Fold in pear slices. Makes about 2 3/4 cups (675 mL) filling. Chill until ready to assemble crêpes.

(continued on next page)

Pear Sauce: Sprinkle gelatin over reserved pear juice in small saucepan. Let stand for 1 minute. Heat and stir on medium until boiling and gelatin is dissolved.

Add margarine. Stir until melted. Add sweetener. Stir. Transfer to small bowl. Cover. Chill for about 30 minutes, stirring occasionally, until slightly cooled. Makes about 1/2 cup (125 mL) sauce. Spoon about 1/3 cup (75 mL) filling along centre of 1 crêpe. Roll up to enclose filling, leaving ends open. Place on medium serving dish. Repeat with remaining crêpes and filling. Drizzle sauce over top. Serves 8.

1 serving: 251 Calories; 20.4 g Total Fat (9 g Mono, 1.7 g Poly, 8.5 g Sat); 118 mg Cholesterol; **12 g Carbohydrate**; 1 g Fibre; 5 g Protein; 191 mg Sodium

Citrus Custards

Low-calorie sweetener helps to keep the carbs low in this luscious lemony dessert.

Large eggs	3	3
Egg yolks (large)	3	3
Low-calorie sweetener (Splenda)	1/2 cup	125 mL
Whipping cream	1/3 cup	75 mL
Orange juice	1/2 cup	125 mL
Lemon juice	1 tbsp.	15 mL

Beat first 4 ingredients in medium bowl until well combined.

Add orange and lemon juices. Beat well. Divide and pour into 4 greased 1/2 cup (125 mL) ovenproof ramekins set in 2 quart (2 L) shallow baking dish. Carefully pour boiling water into baking dish until water comes halfway up sides of ramekins. Bake in 350°F (175°C) oven for about 25 minutes until just set. Custard will still be soft. Remove ramekins from water to wire rack to cool completely. Cover. Chill for at least 6 hours or overnight. Carefully run knife around inside edge of each ramekin to loosen custard. Invert onto 4 individual plates. Serves 4.

1 serving: 192 Calories; 14.4 g Total Fat (4.9 g Mono, 1.3 g Poly, 6.6 g Sat); 347 mg Cholesterol; **5 g Carbohydrate**; trace Fibre; 7 g Protein; 61 mg Sodium

Ginger Custards

Slightly sweet, warm, creamy custard. Crystallized ginger at the bottom of each ramekin adds a pleasant surprise.

Minced crystallized ginger	2 tbsp.	30 mL
Half-and-half cream	1 1/2 cups	375 mL
Coarsely grated, peeled gingerroot	1 tbsp.	15 mL
Large eggs	2	2
Low-calorie sweetener (Splenda)	2 tbsp.	30 mL

Measure about 1/2 tbsp. (7 mL) crystallized ginger into each of 4 greased 1/2 cup (125 mL) ovenproof ramekins set in 2 quart (2 L) shallow baking dish.

Heat cream and grated ginger in medium saucepan on medium until bubbles form around edge. Remove from heat. Cover. Let stand for 30 minutes. Strain cream mixture through sieve into small bowl. Discard solids.

Beat eggs and sweetener with whisk in medium bowl until frothy. Add cream mixture. Beat well. Divide and pour into prepared ramekins. Carefully pour boiling water into baking dish until water comes halfway up sides of ramekins. Bake in 350°F (175°C) oven for about 25 minutes until set and knife inserted in centre of custard comes out clean. Remove ramekins from water to wire rack. Let stand for 5 minutes. Serves 4.

1 serving: 167 Calories; 12.1 g Total Fat (3.7 g Mono, 0.7 g Poly, 6.8 g Sat); 138 mg Cholesterol; **8 g Carbohydrate**; trace Fibre; 6 g Protein; 73 mg Sodium

1. Chocolate Popcorn, page 133
2. Nutty Granola, page 136
3. Lemon Meringue Kisses, page 146

Chocolate Nut Strawberries

Sweet, juicy strawberries dipped in chocolate and coated with almonds. Divinely decadent!

Semi-sweet chocolate baking squares (1 oz., 28 g, each), chopped	**4**	**4**
Large fresh strawberries (with stems), blotted dry	**12**	**12**
Finely chopped natural almonds, toasted (see Tip, page 24)	**1/2 cup**	**125 mL**

Heat chocolate in small heavy saucepan on lowest heat, stirring often, until chocolate is almost melted. Do not overheat. Remove from heat. Stir until smooth. Pour chocolate into custard cup.

Holding 1 strawberry by stem end, dip 2/3 of strawberry straight down into chocolate.

While chocolate is still soft, roll strawberry in almonds in small shallow dish until coated. Place on waxed paper-lined baking sheet. Repeat with remaining strawberries, chocolate and almonds. Chill until chocolate is set. Makes 12 chocolate strawberries.

1 chocolate strawberry: 84 Calories; 5.9 g Total Fat (2.9 g Mono, 0.8 g Poly, 1.9 g Sat); 0 mg Cholesterol; **8 g Carbohydrate**; 1 g Fibre; 2 g Protein; 2 mg Sodium

Pictured on page 144 and on back cover.

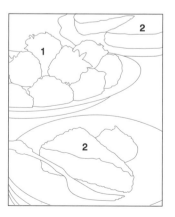

1. Chocolate Nut Strawberries, above
2. Hazelnut Chocolate Torte, page 148

Lemon Meringue Kisses

Delicate meringues bonded together with delicious lemon filling. Greet your family with "kisses"—they will love you for it!

LEMON FILLING

Water	1 tbsp.	15 mL
Cornstarch	1 1/2 tsp.	7 mL
Egg yolks (large)	2	2
Granulated sugar	1/4 cup	60 mL
Lemon juice	1/4 cup	60 mL
Hard margarine (or butter), softened	1/4 cup	60 mL
Grated lemon zest	1 1/2 tsp.	7 mL

MERINGUE KISSES

Egg whites (large)	2	2
Cream of tartar	1/2 tsp.	2 mL
Granulated sugar	1/3 cup	75 mL
Icing (confectioner's) sugar	1/3 cup	75 mL

Lemon Filling: Stir water into cornstarch in small cup until smooth. Set aside.

Combine egg yolks and sugar in small heavy saucepan. Add lemon juice and margarine. Heat and stir on medium-low for 1 to 2 minutes until margarine is melted. Stir cornstarch mixture. Add to lemon mixture, stirring constantly. Heat and stir for about 1 minute until boiling and slightly thickened. Remove from heat.

Add lemon zest. Stir. Transfer to small bowl. Cover with plastic wrap directly on surface to prevent skin from forming. Chill for about 2 hours, stirring occasionally, until cold. Makes about 3/4 cup (175 mL) filling.

Meringue Kisses: Line baking sheets with parchment paper. Beat egg whites and cream of tartar in medium bowl until soft peaks form.

Add granulated sugar, 1 tbsp. (15 mL) at a time while beating, until stiff peaks form and sugar is dissolved.

(continued on next page)

Fold in icing sugar. Spoon meringue into piping bag fitted with large plain tip. Pipe about forty 1/2 inch (12 mm) high by 1 inch (2.5 cm) diameter mounds, lifting tip to create pointed end on each, about 2 inches (5 cm) apart onto parchment paper. Bake on bottom rack in 225°F (110°C) oven for about 45 minutes until dry. Turn oven off. Let stand in oven until cooled completely. Spoon lemon filling into separate piping bag fitted with plain medium tip. Pipe about 2 tsp. (10 mL) filling onto bottom of 1 meringue. Press bottom of second meringue onto filling. Repeat with remaining meringues and filling. Makes about 20 meringue kisses.

1 meringue kiss: 63 Calories; 2.9 g Total Fat (1.8 g Mono, 0.3 g Poly, 0.7 g Sat); 22 mg Cholesterol; **9 g Carbohydrate**; trace Fibre; 1 g Protein; 35 mg Sodium

Pictured on page 143.

Baked Berry Peaches

A different way to serve fruit for dessert. Almonds add a bit of crunch.

Chopped fresh strawberries	**1 1/2 cups**	**375 mL**
Low-calorie sweetener (Splenda)	**2 tbsp.**	**30 mL**
Large fresh peaches, halved, pitted	**4**	**4**
Hard margarine (or butter), cut up	**2 tbsp.**	**30 mL**
Low-calorie sweetener (Splenda)	**2 tbsp.**	**30 mL**
Orange-flavoured liqueur (such as Grand Marnier), optional	**1 tbsp.**	**15 mL**
Sliced almonds, toasted (see Tip, page 24)	**2 tbsp.**	**30 mL**

Combine strawberries and first amount of sweetener in small bowl. Spread evenly in greased 2 quart (2 L) shallow baking dish.

Arrange peach halves, cut-side up, on top of strawberries. Scatter margarine over peaches. Sprinkle second amount of sweetener over top. Bake in 400°F (205°C) oven for about 20 minutes until peaches are just tender.

Drizzle liqueur over peaches. Sprinkle with almonds. Serves 8.

1 serving: 71 Calories; 3.9 g Total Fat (2.5 g Mono, 0.6 g Poly, 0.7 g Sat); 0 mg Cholesterol; **8 g Carbohydrate**; 2 g Fibre; 1 g Protein; 34 mg Sodium

Hazelnut Chocolate Torte

Distinct thin layers make this light, not-too-sweet dessert an attractive choice for company.

HAZELNUT CRUST		
Finely chopped hazelnuts (filberts), toasted (see Tip, page 24)	**1 cup**	**250 mL**
Hard margarine (or butter), melted	**1/4 cup**	**60 mL**
CHOCOLATE FILLING		
Unsweetened chocolate baking squares (1 oz., 28 g, each), chopped	**2**	**2**
Hard margarine (or butter)	**3 tbsp.**	**50 mL**
Low-calorie sweetener (Splenda)	**1/3 cup**	**75 mL**
Whipping cream	**1/4 cup**	**60 mL**
Vanilla	**1/2 tsp.**	**2 mL**
HAZELNUT CHEESE FILLING		
Block of light cream cheese, softened	**8 oz.**	**250 g**
Low-calorie sweetener (Splenda)	**1/3 cup**	**75 mL**
Ground hazelnuts (filberts), toasted (see Tip, page 24)	**1/3 cup**	**75 mL**
COCOA CREAM		
Whipping cream	**3/4 cup**	**175 mL**
Cocoa, sifted if lumpy	**1 tbsp.**	**15 mL**
Low-calorie sweetener (Splenda)	**1 tbsp.**	**15 mL**
Vanilla	**1 tsp.**	**5 mL**
Cocoa, sifted if lumpy	**1 tsp.**	**5 mL**
Finely chopped hazelnuts (filberts), toasted (see Tip, page 24), for garnish	**2 tsp.**	**10 mL**

Hazelnut Crust: Combine hazelnuts and margarine in small bowl. Press firmly in bottom of greased 8 inch (20 cm) springform pan. Place in freezer until cold.

Chocolate Filling: Heat chocolate and margarine in small saucepan on lowest heat, stirring often, until chocolate is almost melted. Do not overheat. Remove from heat. Stir until smooth. Add sweetener, whipping cream and vanilla. Stir well. Makes about 1/2 cup (125 mL) filling. Spread evenly over crust. Freeze until set.

Hazelnut Cheese Filling: Beat cream cheese in medium bowl until smooth. Add sweetener and hazelnuts. Beat well. Makes about 1 cup (250 mL) filling. Spread evenly over chocolate layer. Place in freezer until cold.

Cocoa Cream: Beat first 4 ingredients in small bowl until stiff peaks form. Makes about 1 1/3 cups (325 mL) cream. Spread evenly over cream cheese layer.

(continued on next page)

Dust with second amount of cocoa. Garnish with hazelnuts. Cover. Chill for at least 4 hours until cold. Cuts into 8 wedges.

1 wedge: 437 Calories; 43.3 g Total Fat (22.9 g Mono, 3 g Poly, 15.3 g Sat); 56 mg Cholesterol; **8 g Carbohydrate**; 3 g Fibre; 7 g Protein; 353 mg Sodium

Pictured on page 144 and on back cover.

Pumpkin Pie

Nothing says comfort like the aroma of pumpkin pie! A pecan crust cuts the carbs in this sumptuous version.

PECAN CRUST

Finely chopped pecans, toasted (see Tip, page 24)	**1 cup**	**250 mL**
Hard margarine (or butter), melted	**1 tbsp.**	**15 mL**

PUMPKIN FILLING

Large eggs	**3**	**3**
Low-calorie sweetener (Splenda)	**1/2 cup**	**125 mL**
Can of pure pumpkin (no spices)	**14 oz.**	**398 mL**
Half-and-half cream	**1 1/4 cups**	**300 mL**
Ground cinnamon	**1/2 tsp.**	**2 mL**
Ground nutmeg	**1/2 tsp.**	**2 mL**
Salt	**1/4 tsp.**	**1 mL**

Icing (confectioner's) sugar, for dusting (optional)

Pecan Crust: Combine pecans and margarine in small bowl. Press firmly in bottom of 9 inch (22 cm) pie plate. Chill until firm.

Pumpkin Filling: Beat eggs and sweetener in medium bowl until thick and pale.

Add next 5 ingredients. Beat well. Makes about 3 1/2 cups (875 mL) filling. Spread evenly over crust. Bake in 350°F (175°C) oven for about 50 minutes until set and knife inserted in centre comes out clean. Cool completely.

Dust with icing sugar. Cuts into 8 wedges.

1 wedge: 216 Calories; 18 g Total Fat (9.4 g Mono, 3.2 g Poly, 4.3 g Sat); 93 mg Cholesterol; **9 g Carbohydrate**; 2 g Fibre; 5 g Protein; 134 mg Sodium

Measurement Tables

Throughout this book measurements are given in Conventional and Metric measure. To compensate for differences between the two measurements due to rounding, a full metric measure is not always used. The cup used is the standard 8 fluid ounce. Temperature is given in degrees Fahrenheit and Celsius. Baking pan measurements are in inches and centimetres as well as quarts and litres. An exact metric conversion is given below as well as the working equivalent (Standard Measure).

OVEN TEMPERATURES

Fahrenheit (°F)	Celsius (°C)
175°	80°
200°	95°
225°	110°
250°	120°
275°	140°
300°	150°
325°	160°
350°	175°
375°	190°
400°	205°
425°	220°
450°	230°
475°	240°
500°	260°

SPOONS

Conventional Measure	Metric Exact Conversion Millilitre (mL)	Metric Standard Measure Millilitre (mL)
1/8 teaspoon (tsp.)	0.6 mL	0.5 mL
1/4 teaspoon (tsp.)	1.2 mL	1 mL
1/2 teaspoon (tsp.)	2.4 mL	2 mL
1 teaspoon (tsp.)	4.7 mL	5 mL
2 teaspoons (tsp.)	9.4 mL	10 mL
1 tablespoon (tbsp.)	14.2 mL	15 mL

CUPS

1/4 cup (4 tbsp.)	56.8 mL	60 mL
1/3 cup (5 1/3 tbsp.)	75.6 mL	75 mL
1/2 cup (8 tbsp.)	113.7 mL	125 mL
2/3 cup (10 2/3 tbsp.)	151.2 mL	150 mL
3/4 cup (12 tbsp.)	170.5 mL	175 mL
1 cup (16 tbsp.)	227.3 mL	250 mL
4 1/2 cups	1022.9 mL	1000 mL (1 L)

PANS

Conventional Inches	Metric Centimetres
8x8 inch	20x20 cm
9x9 inch	22x22 cm
9x13 inch	22x33 cm
10x15 inch	25x38 cm
11x17 inch	28x43 cm
8x2 inch round	20x5 cm
9x2 inch round	22x5 cm
10x4 1/2 inch tube	25x11 cm
8x4x3 inch loaf	20x10x7.5 cm
9x5x3 inch loaf	22x12.5x7.5 cm

DRY MEASUREMENTS

Conventional Measure Ounces (oz.)	Metric Exact Conversion Grams (g)	Metric Standard Measure Grams (g)
1 oz.	28.3 g	28 g
2 oz.	56.7 g	57 g
3 oz.	85.0 g	85 g
4 oz.	113.4 g	125 g
5 oz.	141.7 g	140 g
6 oz.	170.1 g	170 g
7 oz.	198.4 g	200 g
8 oz.	226.8 g	250 g
16 oz.	453.6 g	500 g
32 oz.	907.2 g	1000 g (1 kg)

CASSEROLES (Canada & Britain)

Standard Size Casserole	Exact Metric Measure
1 qt. (5 cups)	1.13 L
1 1/2 qts. (7 1/2 cups)	1.69 L
2 qts. (10 cups)	2.25 L
2 1/2 qts. (12 1/2 cups)	2.81 L
3 qts. (15 cups)	3.38 L
4 qts. (20 cups)	4.5 L
5 qts. (25 cups)	5.63 L

CASSEROLES (United States)

Standard Size Casserole	Exact Metric Measure
1 qt. (4 cups)	900 mL
1 1/2 qts. (6 cups)	1.35 L
2 qts. (8 cups)	1.8 L
2 1/2 qts. (10 cups)	2.25 L
3 qts. (12 cups)	2.7 L
4 qts. (16 cups)	3.6 L
5 qts. (20 cups)	4.5 L

Recipe Index

D

Mail Order Form

See reverse for list of cookbooks

EXCLUSIVE MAIL ORDER OFFER
Buy 2 Get 1 FREE!
Buy any 2 cookbooks—choose a **3rd FREE**
of equal or less value than the lowest price paid.

QUANTITY	CODE	TITLE	PRICE EACH	PRICE TOTAL
			$	$
	TOTAL BOOKS (including FREE)			

DON'T FORGET to indicate your FREE book(s) (see exclusive mail order offer above) PLEASE PRINT

TOTAL BOOKS PURCHASED: $

	INTERNATIONAL	CANADA & USA
Plus Shipping & Handling (PER DESTINATION)	$ 11.98 (one book)	$ 5.98 (one book)
Additional Books (INCLUDING FREE BOOKS)	$ ($4.99 each)	$ ($1.99 each)
SUB-TOTAL	$	$
Canadian residents add G.S.T.(7%)		$
TOTAL AMOUNT ENCLOSED	$	$

The Fine Print

- Orders outside Canada must be **PAID IN US FUNDS** by cheque or money order drawn on Canadian or US bank or by credit card.
- Make cheque or money order payable to: **Company's Coming Publishing Limited.**
- Prices are expressed in Canadian dollars for Canada, US dollars for USA & International and are subject to change without prior notice.
- Orders are shipped surface mail. For courier rates, visit our website: **www.companyscoming.com** or contact us: Tel: 780-450-6223 Fax 780-450-1857.
- Sorry, no C.O.D.'s

☐ MasterCard   ☐ VISA

Expiry date

Account #

Name of cardholder

Cardholder's signature

Shipping Address

Send the cookbooks listed above to:

Name:

Street:

City: Prov./State:

Postal Code/Zip: Country:

Tel: (   )

E-mail address:

☐ YES! Please send a catalogue

Gift Giving

- Let us help you with your gift giving!
- We will send cookbooks directly to the recipients of your choice if you give us their names and addresses.
- Please specify the titles you wish to send to each person.
- If you would like to include your personal note or card, we will be pleased to enclose it with your gift order.
- Company's Coming Cookbooks make excellent gifts: birthdays, bridal showers, Mother's Day, Father's Day, graduation or any occasion... collect them all!

Company's Coming ®

Canada's most **popular cookbooks**